Creative Movie Posters Color by Number Mosaic Movie Images and Scenes Adult Coloring Book Movies to Color for Stress Relief and Relaxation

By Color Questopia

Copyright © 2020

All rights reserved. No part of this publication may be reproduced, distributed, or transmitted in any form or by any means, including photocopying, recording, or other electronic or mechanical methods, without the prior written permission of the publisher

1. Black
2. Dark Brown
3. Peach
4. Brown
5. Medium Brown
6. Light Brown
7. Red
8. Orange
9. Dark Orange
10. Blue
11. Dark Blue
12. Light Violet
13. Yellow
14. Green
15. Dark Yellow
16. Gray
17. Light Blue
18. Navy Blue

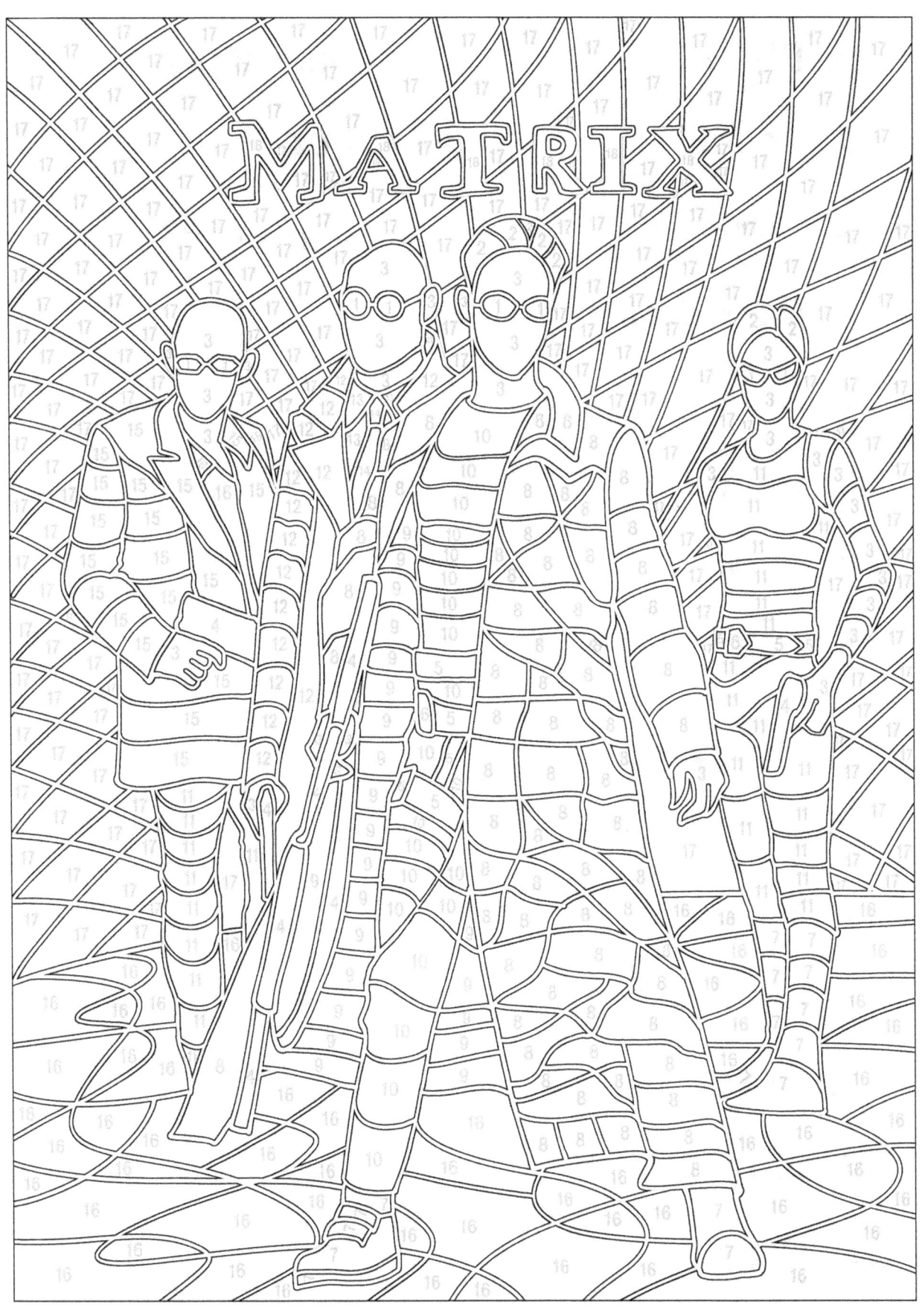

1. Black
2. Peach
3. Violet
4. Dark Violet
5. Blue
6. Navy Blue
7. Pink
8. Light Pink
9. Orange
10. Dark Orange
11. Yellow
12. Light Brown
13. Brown
14. Light Gray
15. Gray
16. Dark Gray
17. Red
18. Light Blue

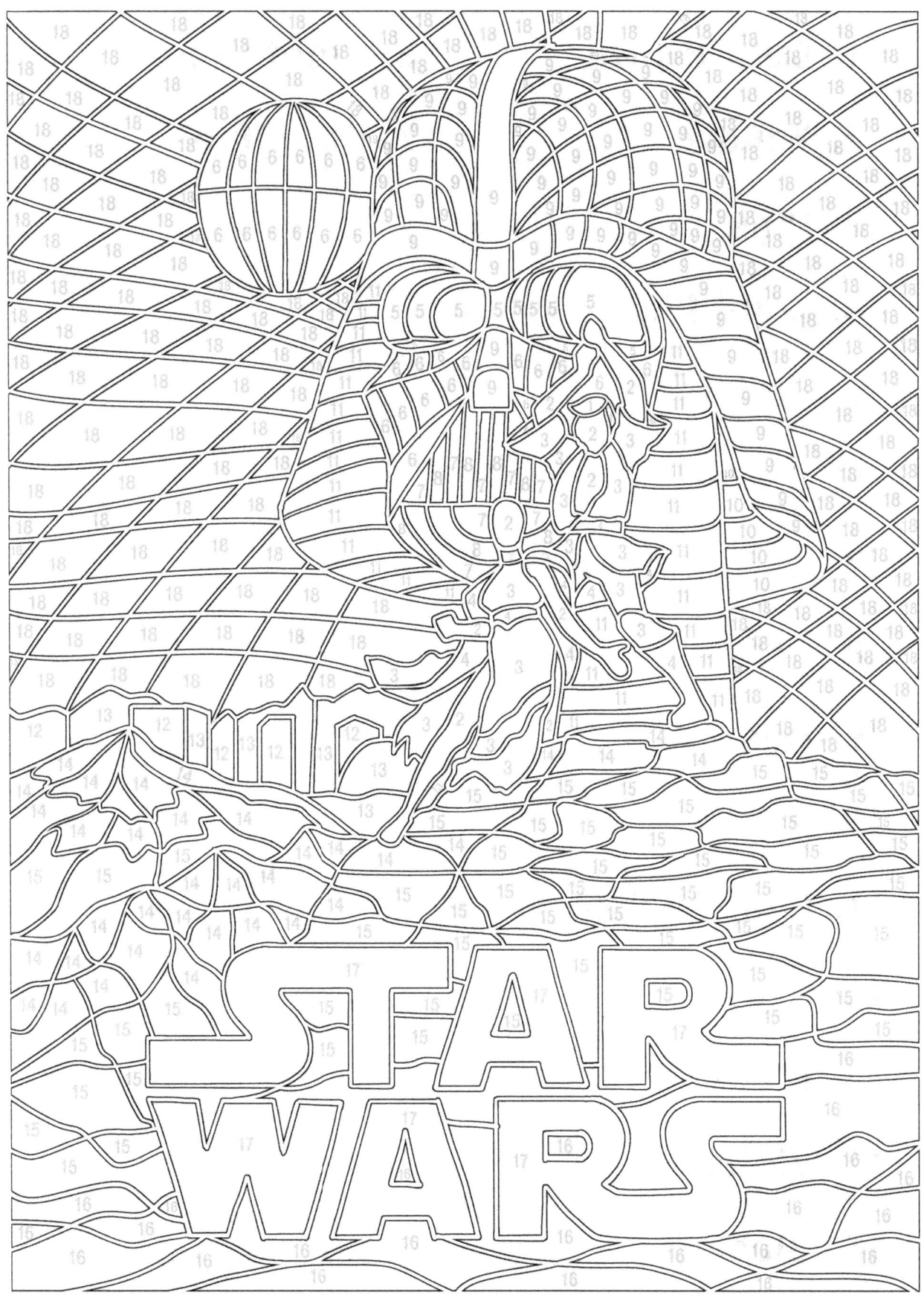

1. Dark Brown
2. Yellow
3. Pink
4. Light Pink
5. Violet
6. Orange
7. Dark Orange
8. Brown
9. Red
10. Peach
11. Light Violet
12. Green
13. Black
14. Violet
15. Blue
16. Light Blue
17. Sky Blue

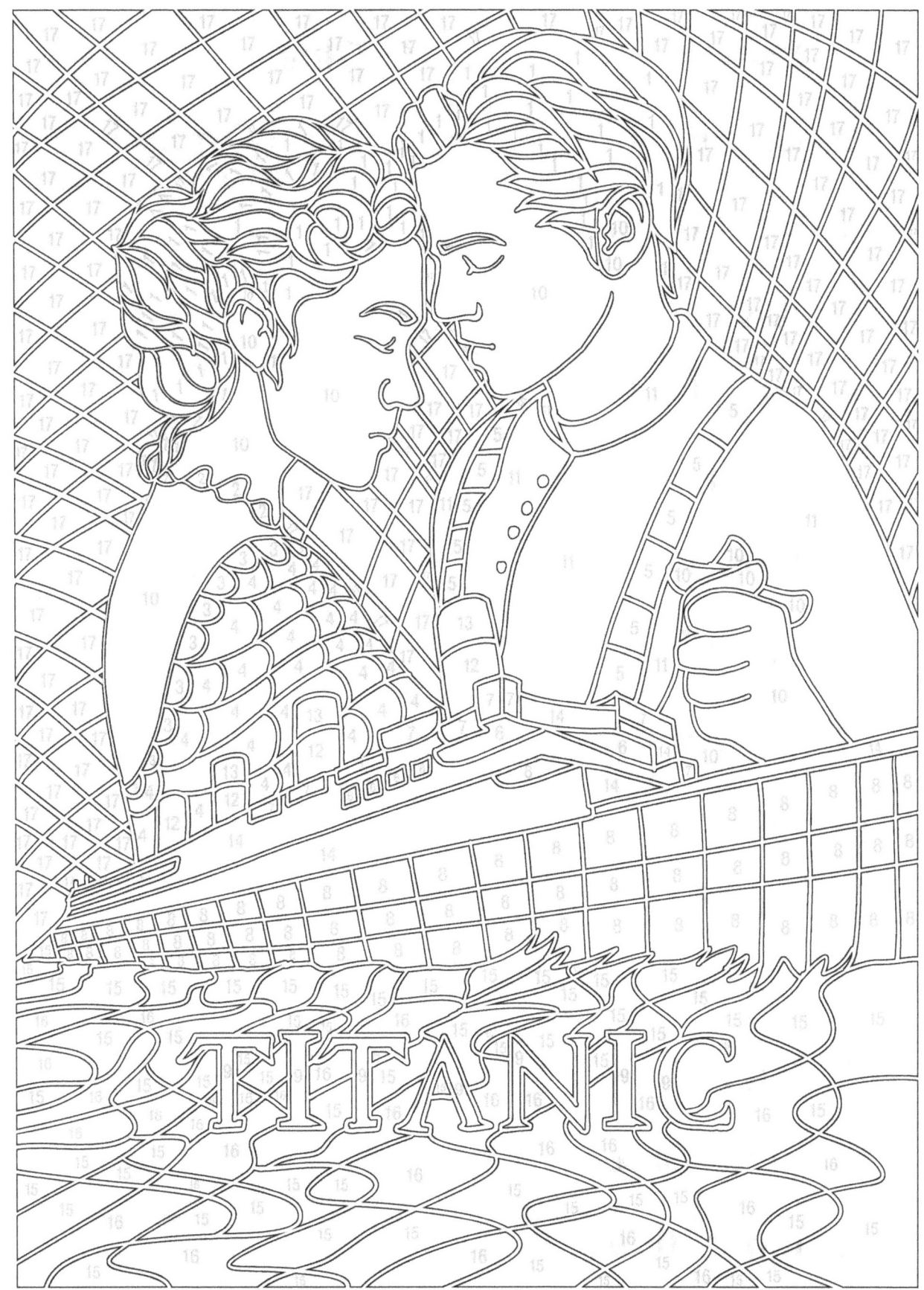

1. Brown
2. Orange
3. Dark Brown
4. Red
5. Dark Red
6. Black
7. Pink
8. Light Violet
9. Navy Blue
10. Violet
11. Peach
12. Yellow
13. Light Pink
14. Light Green
15. Light Blue
16. Blue
17. Light Orange

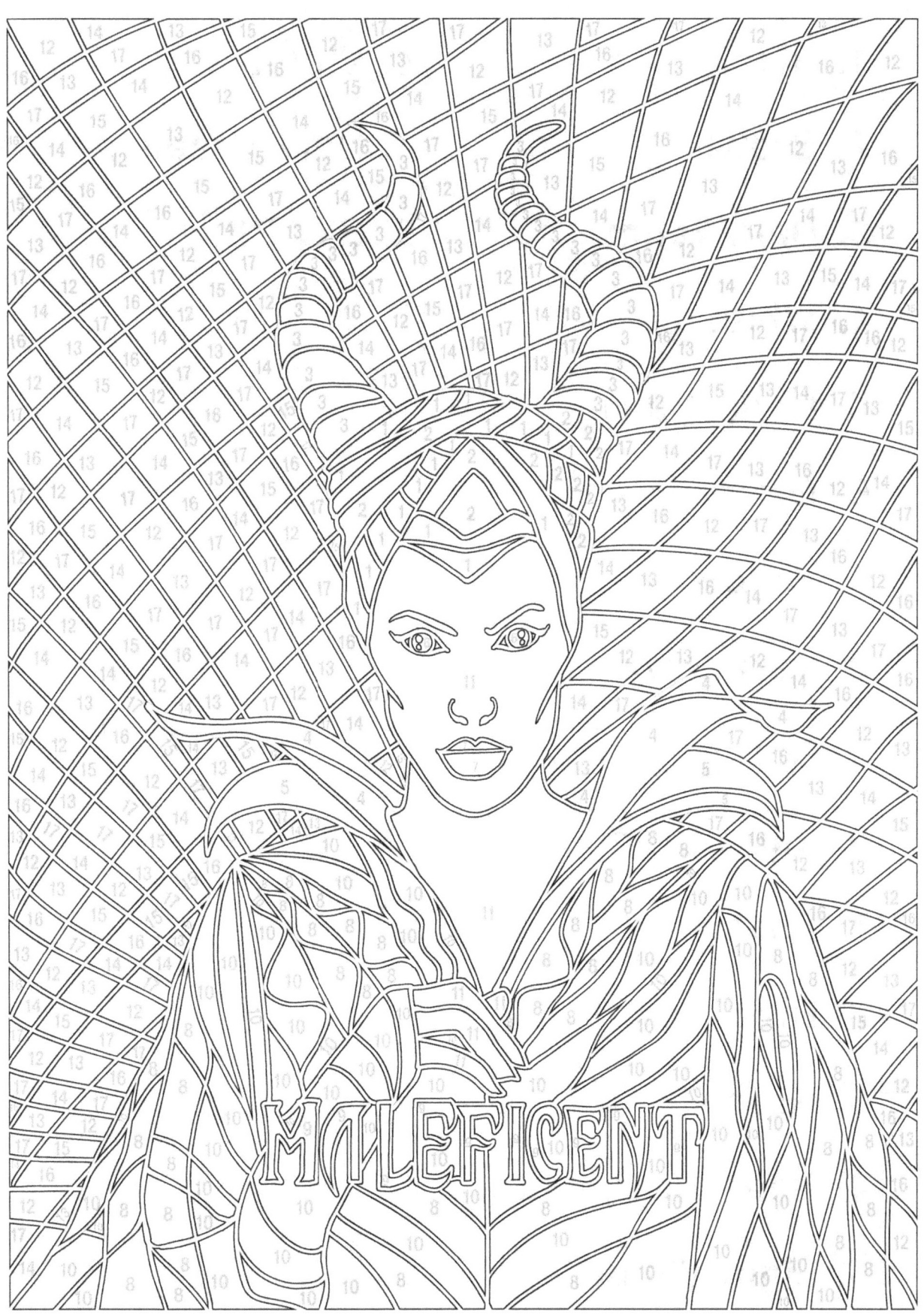

1. Black
2. Brown
3. Dark Yellow
4. White
5. Dark Brown
6. Gray
7. Yellow
8. Dark Gray
9. Orange
10. Light Orange
11. Peach
12. Blue
13. Green
14. Red
15. Light Violet
16. Violet
17. Dark Green
18. Sky Blue

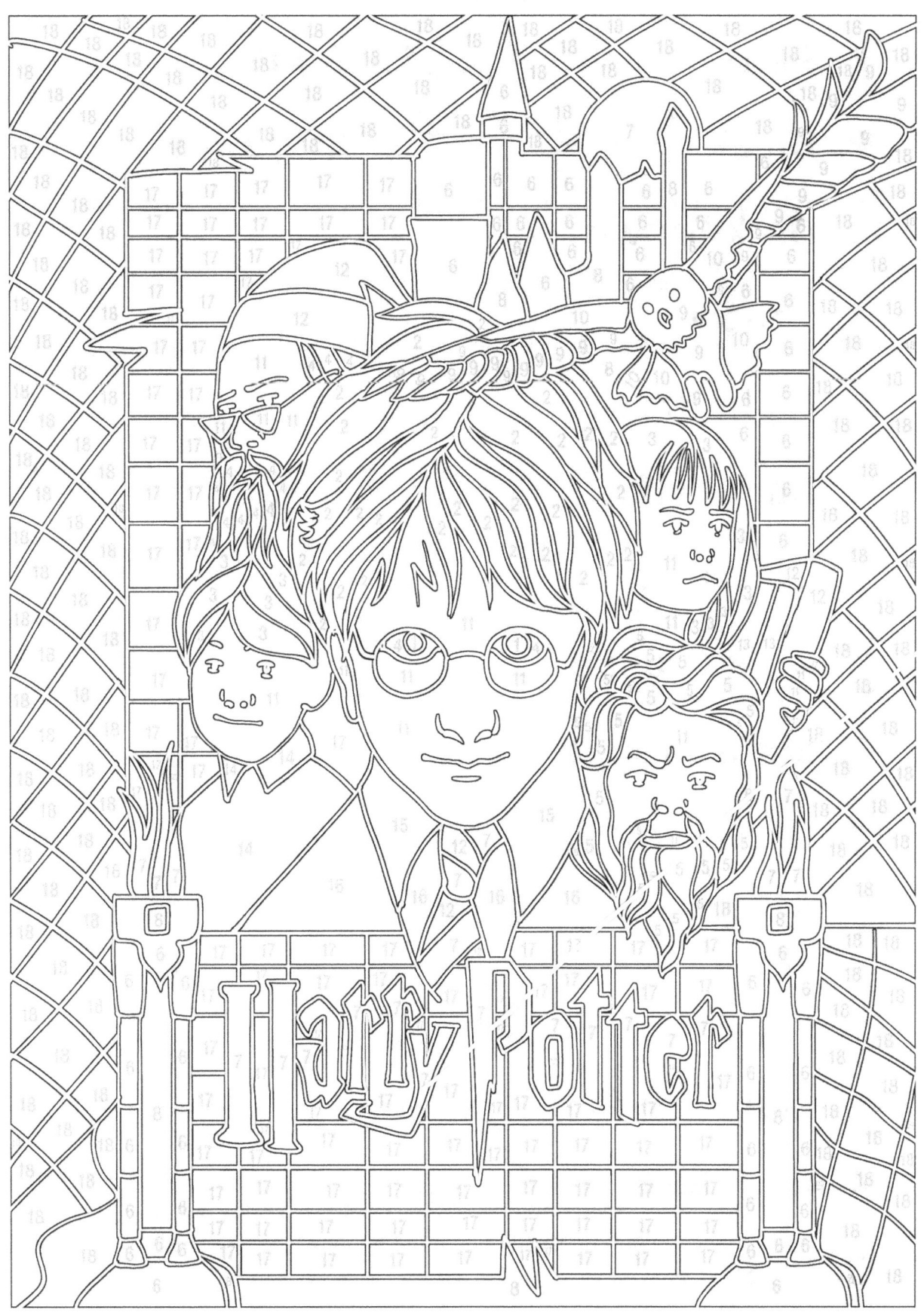

1. Red
2. Black
3. Dark Brown
4. Yellow
5. Light Brown
6. Dark Yellow
7. Dark Red
8. Dark Orange
9. Light Orange
10. Brown
11. Green
12. Orange
13. Light Violet
14. Dark Blue
15. Peach
16. Sky Blue
17. Baby Blue

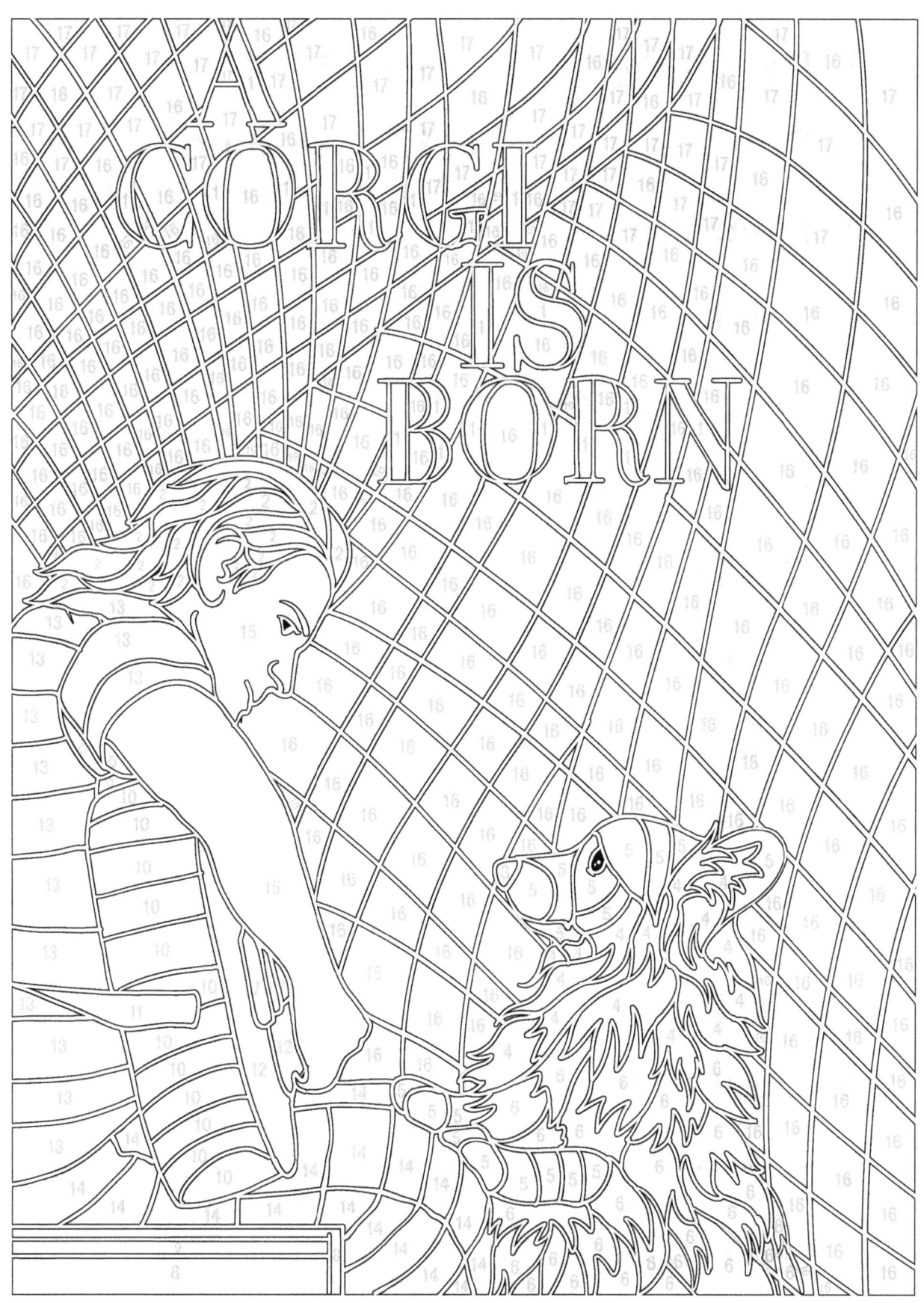

1. Dark Brown
2. Brown
3. Light Brown
4. Black
5. Light Orange
6. Dark Orange
7. Orange
8. Dark Blue
9. Red
10. Violet
11. Yellow
12. Neon Green
13. Light Green
14. Peach
15. Dark Green
16. Green
17. Sky Blue

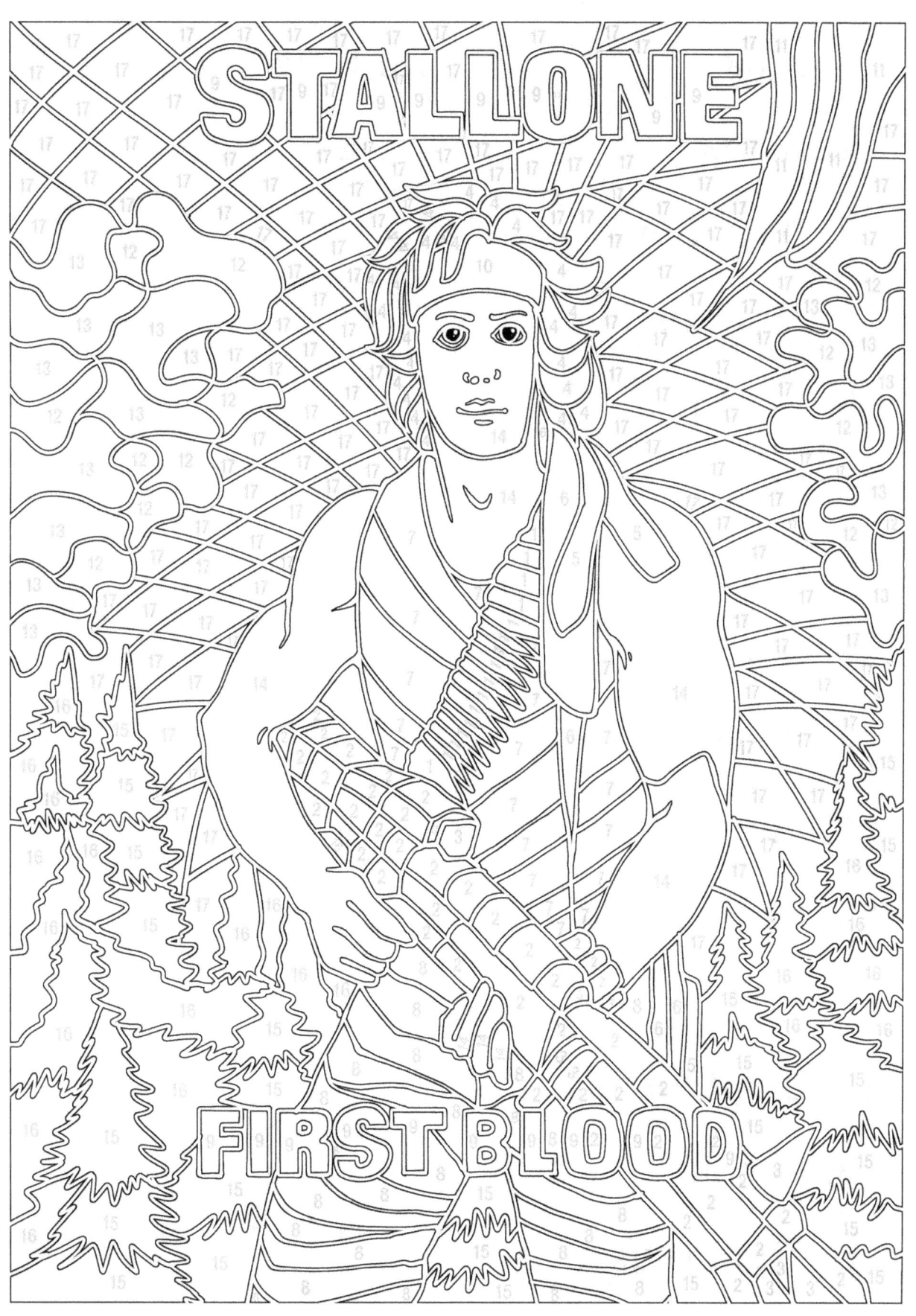

1. Pink
2. Black
3. Dark Brown
4. Light Pink
5. Orange
6. White
7. Green
8. Red
9. Yellow
10. Violet
11. Neon Green
12. Brown
13. Light Violet
14. Peach
15. Light Blue
16. Blue
17. Sky Blue

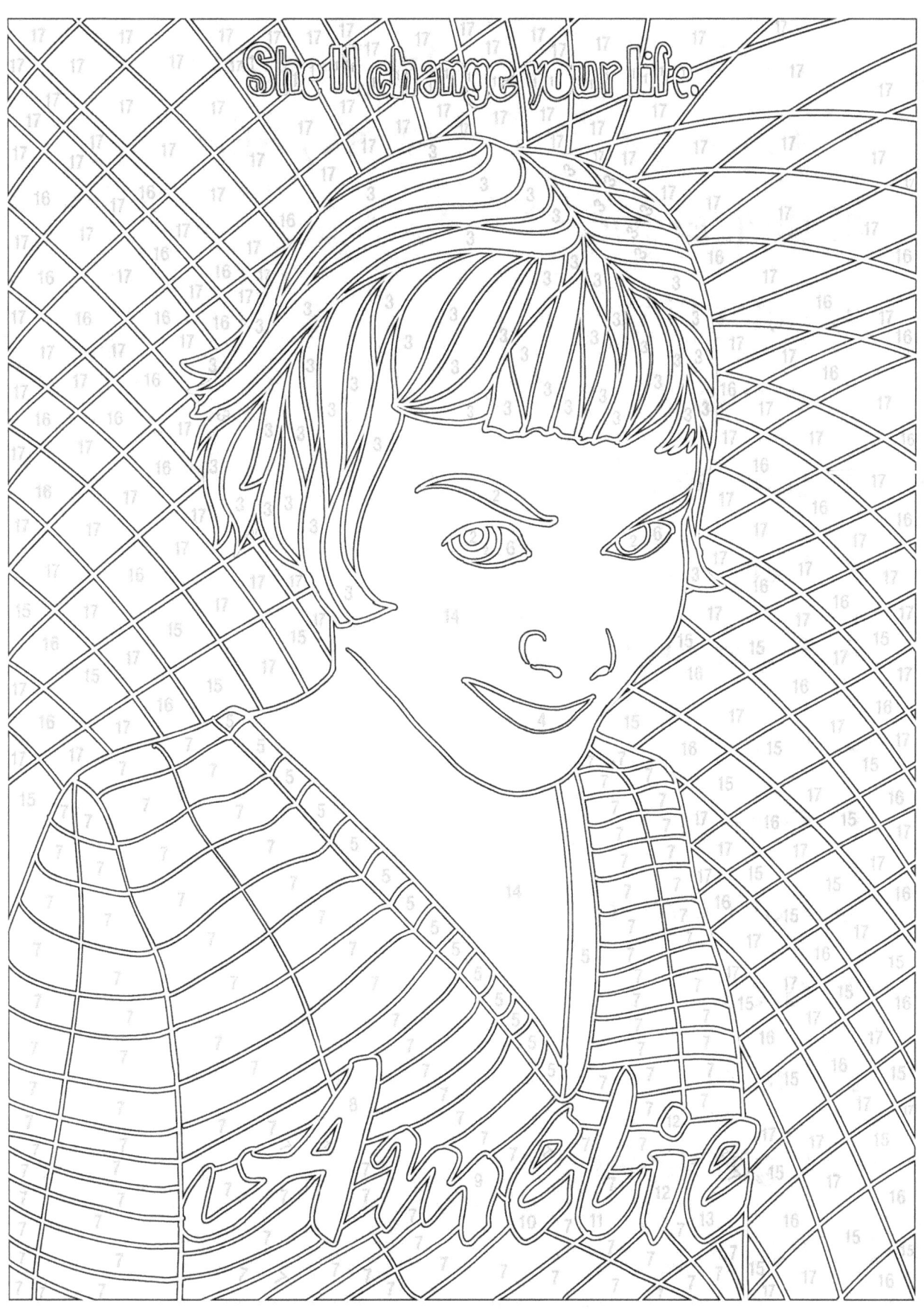

1. Black
2. White
3. Dark Brown
4. Light Pink
5. Yellow
6. Dark Red
7. Red
8. Light Brown
9. Brown
10. Orange
11. Dark Green
12. Green
13. Violet
14. Light Violet
15. Peach
16. Dark Blue
17. Sky Blue

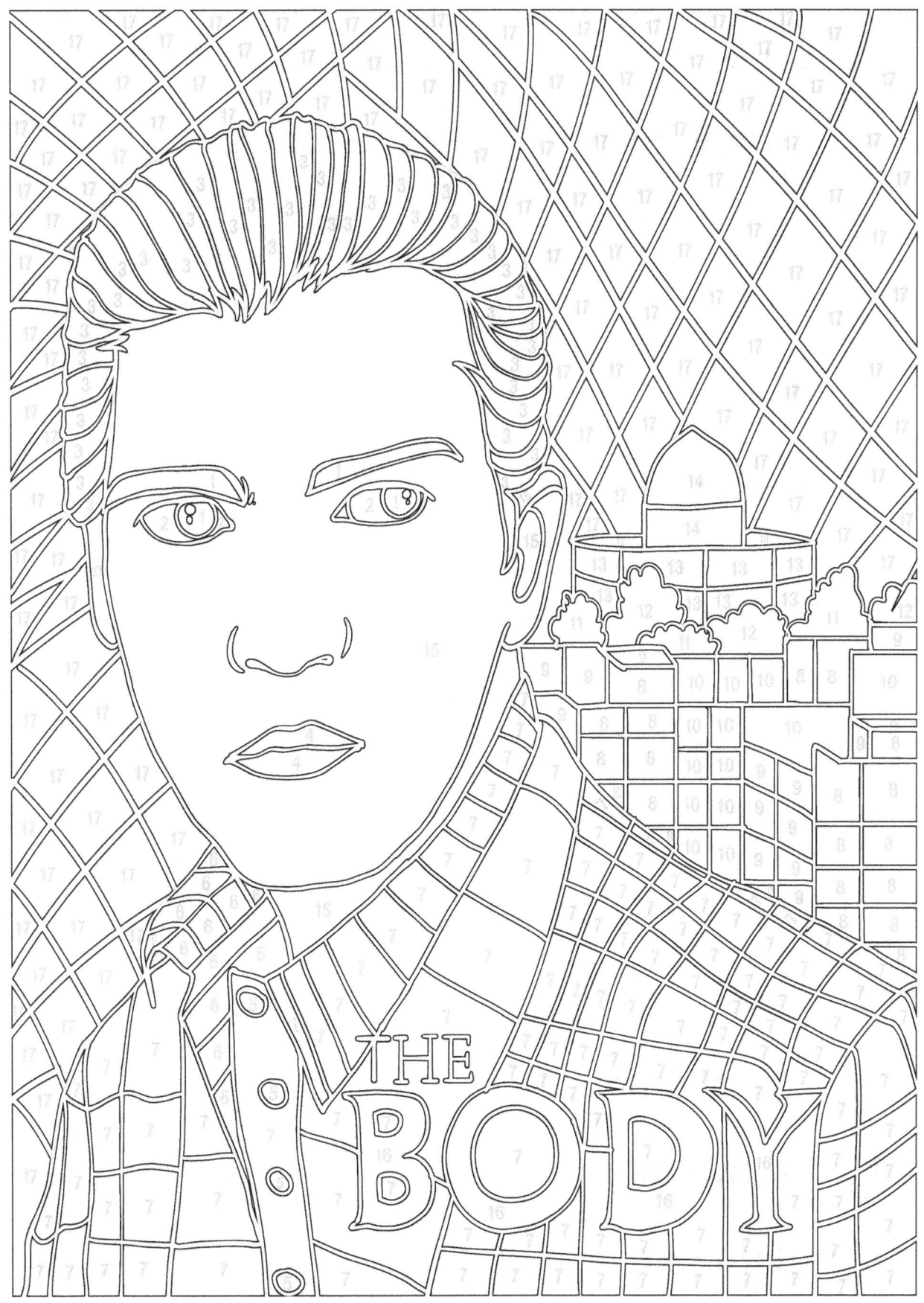

1. Blue
2. Dark Brown
3. Black
4. White
5. Red
6. Yellow
7. Light Brown
8. Violet
9. Light Orange
10. Orange
11. Peach
12. Green
13. Light Violet
14. Light Pink
15. Neon Green
16. Light Blue
17. Baby Blue

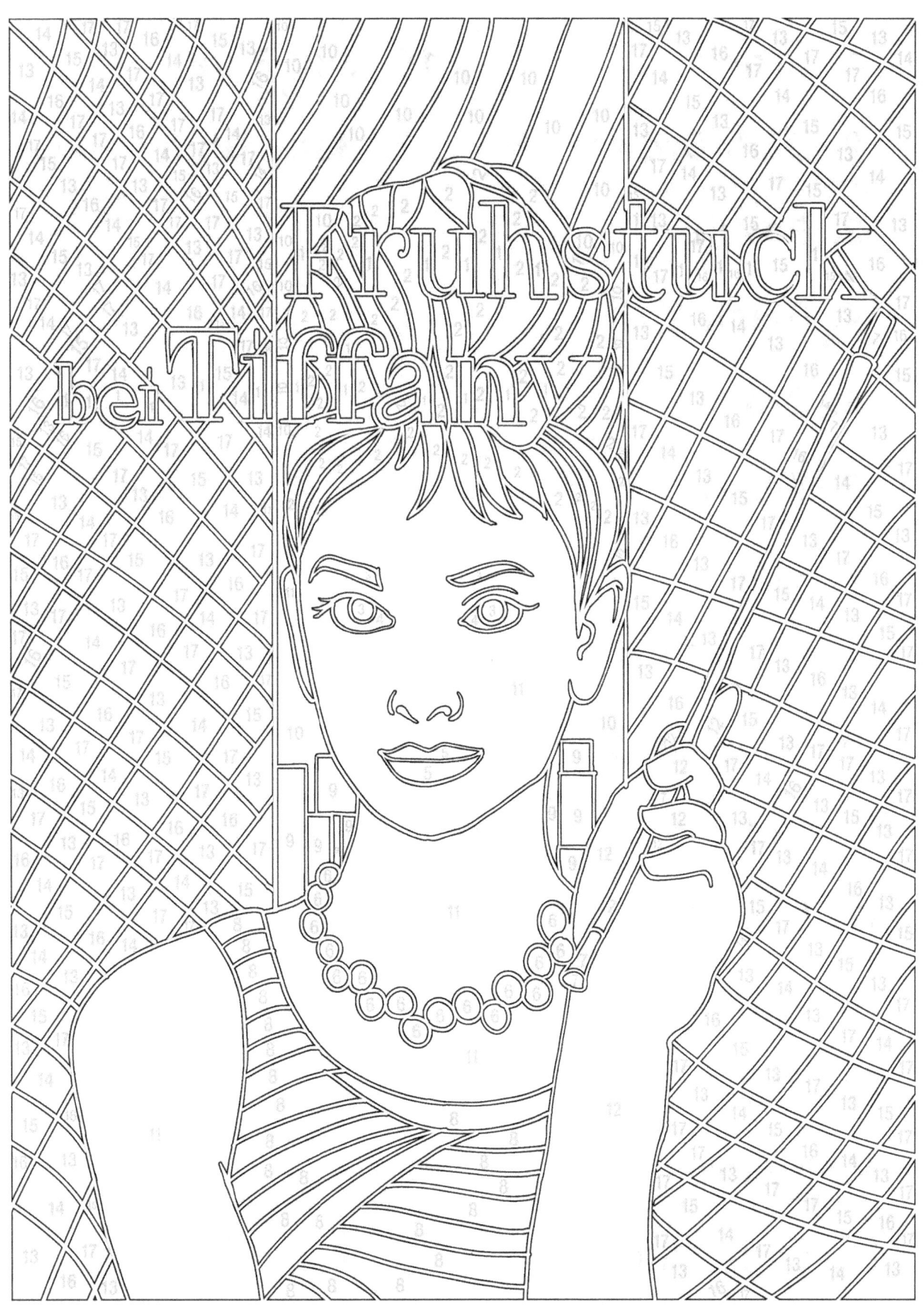

1. Brown
2. Dark Brown
3. Peach
4. Black
5. Orange
6. Violet
7. Pink
8. Light Pink
9. Neon Green
10. Gray
11. Light Gray
12. Dark Blue
13. Red
14. Yellow
15. Light Blue
16. Sky Blue
17. Baby Blue

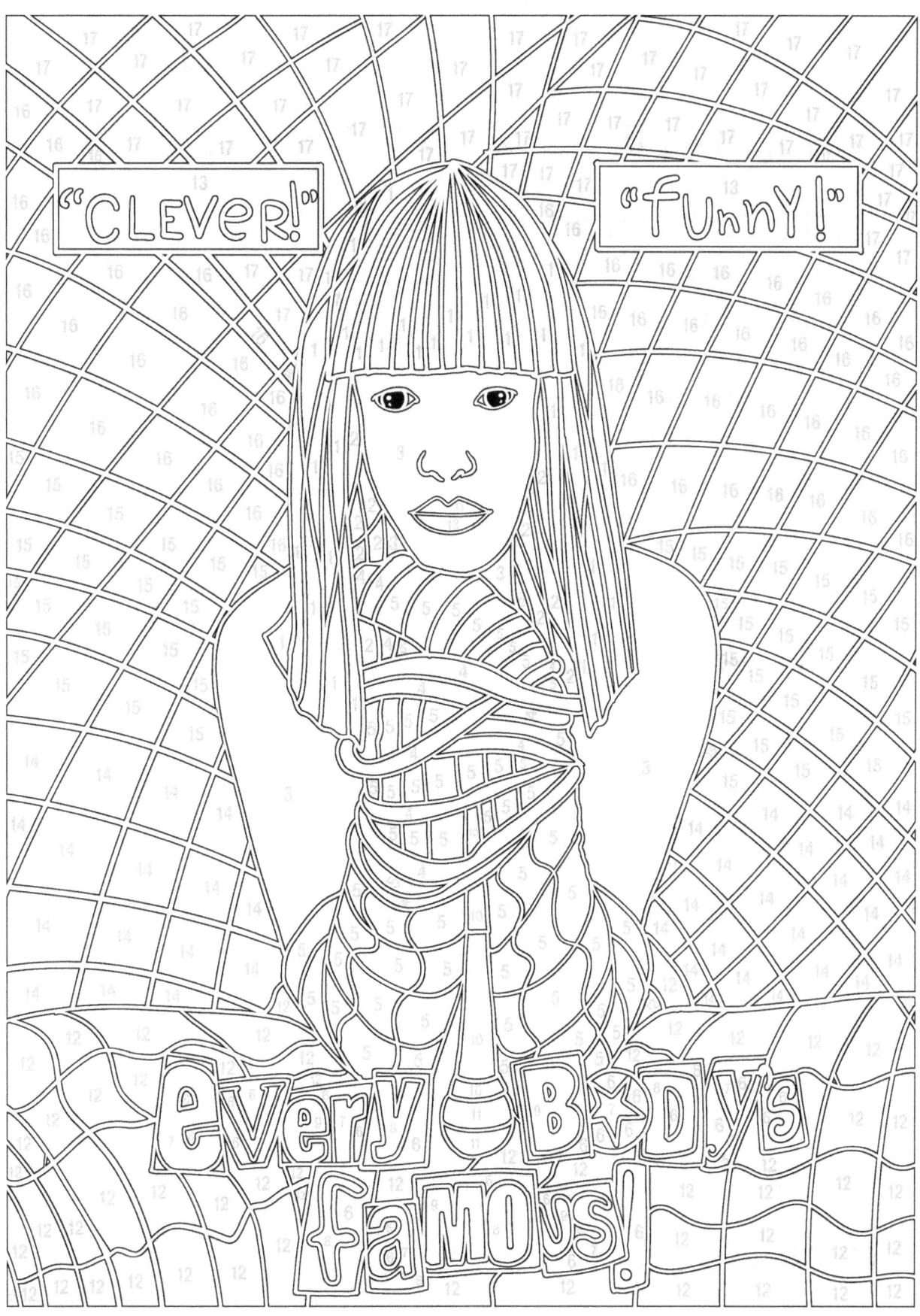

1. Black
2. Light Pink
3. Light Brown
4. Brown
5. Dark Red
6. Blue
7. Green
8. Violet
9. Orange
10. Light Violet
11. Dark Brown
12. Peach
13. Navy Blue
14. Red
15. Sky Blue
16. Light Blue
17. Baby Blue

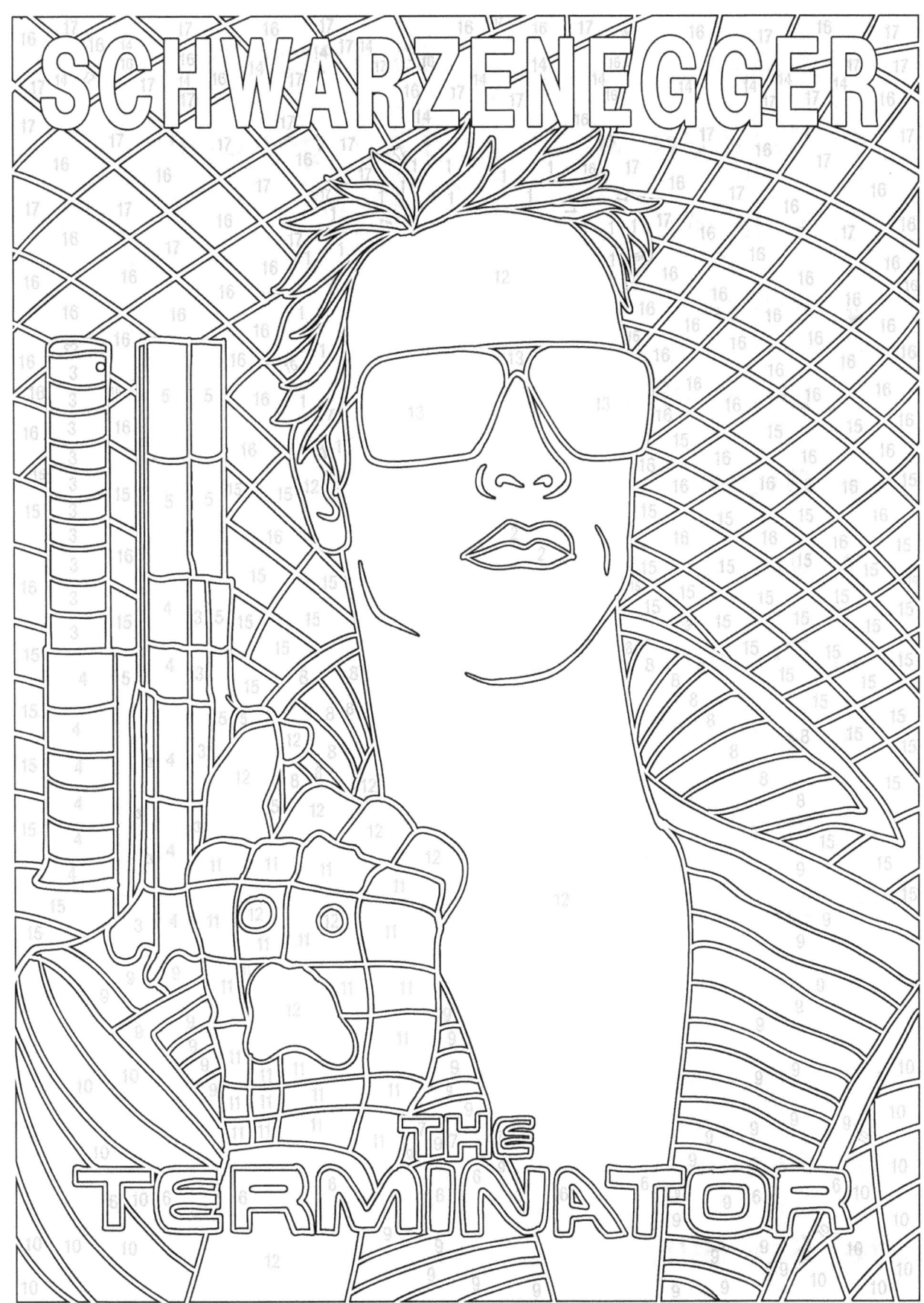

1. Black
2. Dark Brown
3. Yellow
4. White
5. Light Pink
6. Green
7. Violet
8. Orange
9. Red
10. Blue
11. Brown
12. Pink
13. Light Violet
14. Peach
15. Sky Blue
16. Baby Blue
17. Light Gray

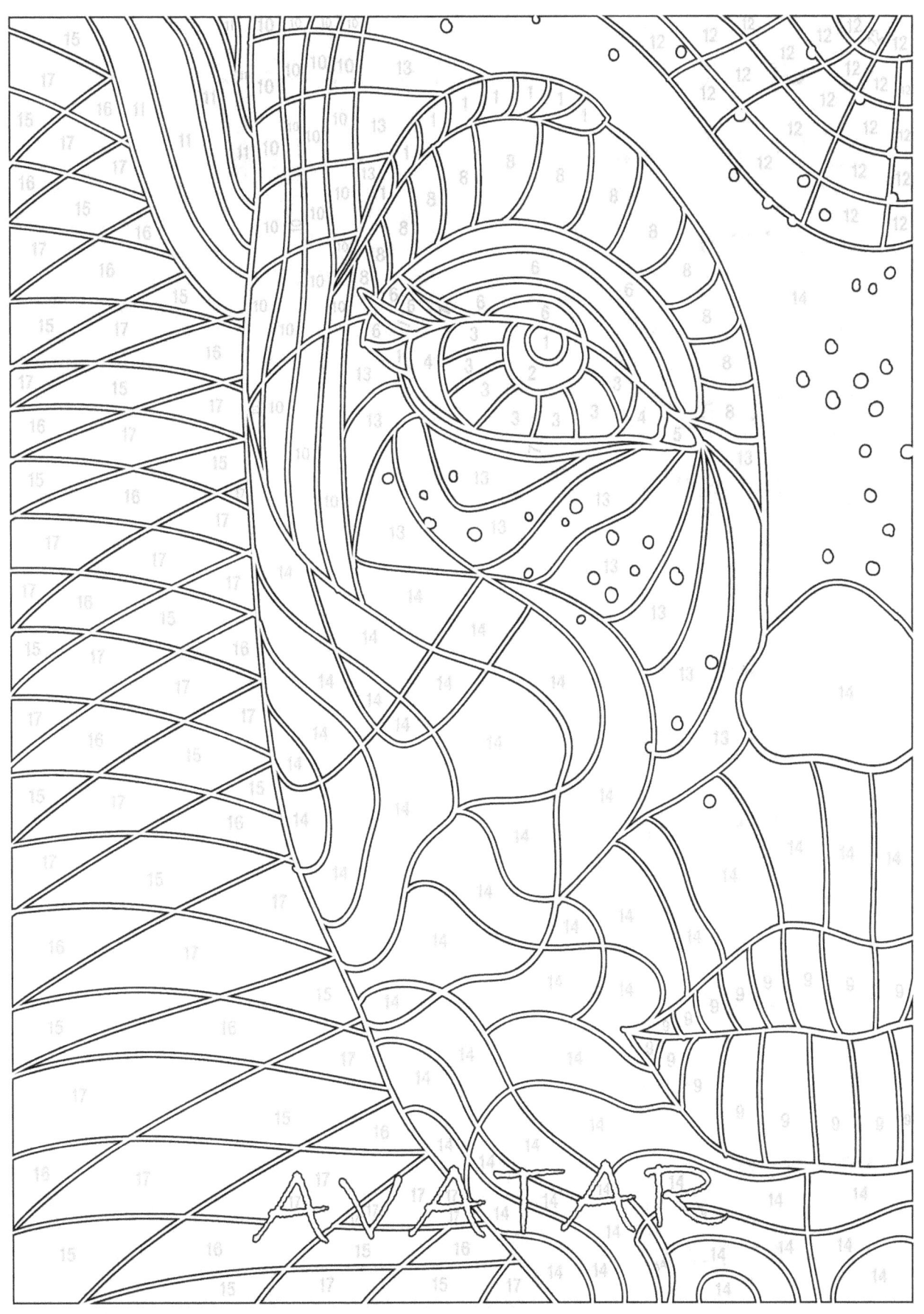

1. Black
2. Light Pink
3. Brown
4. Dark Brown
5. White
6. Light Gray
7. Dark Yellow
8. Gray
9. Dark Orange
10. Light Brown
11. Peach
12. Green
13. Dark Green
14. Red
15. Yellow
16. Sky Blue
17. Light Blue

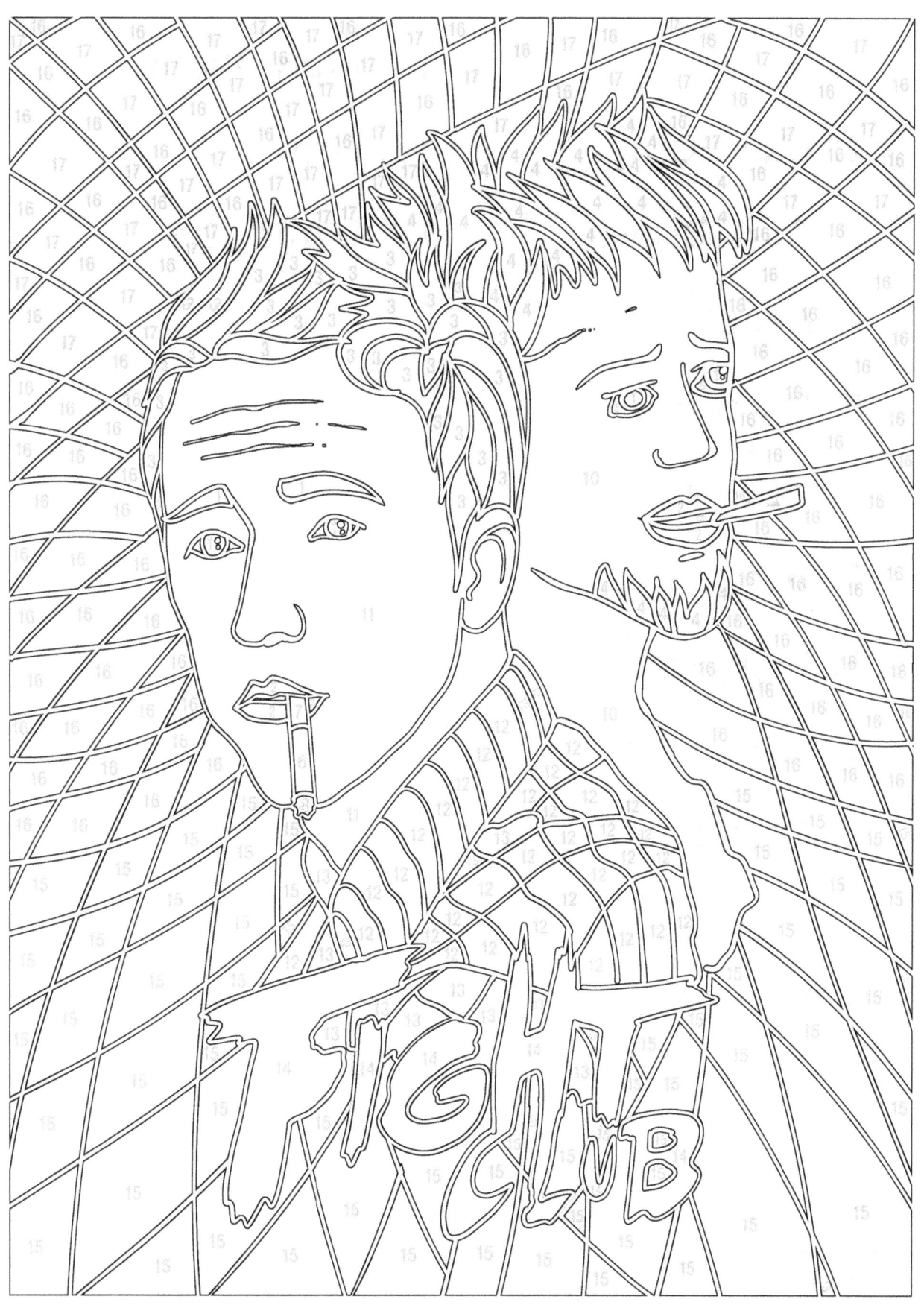

1. Green
2. Light Gray
3. Dark Brown
4. Peach
5. Light Brown
6. Yellow
7. Dark Yellow
8. Light Orange
9. Dark Blue
10. Orange
11. Black
12. Light Pink
13. Pink
14. Brown
15. Violet
16. Light Violet
17. Gray
18. Light Blue

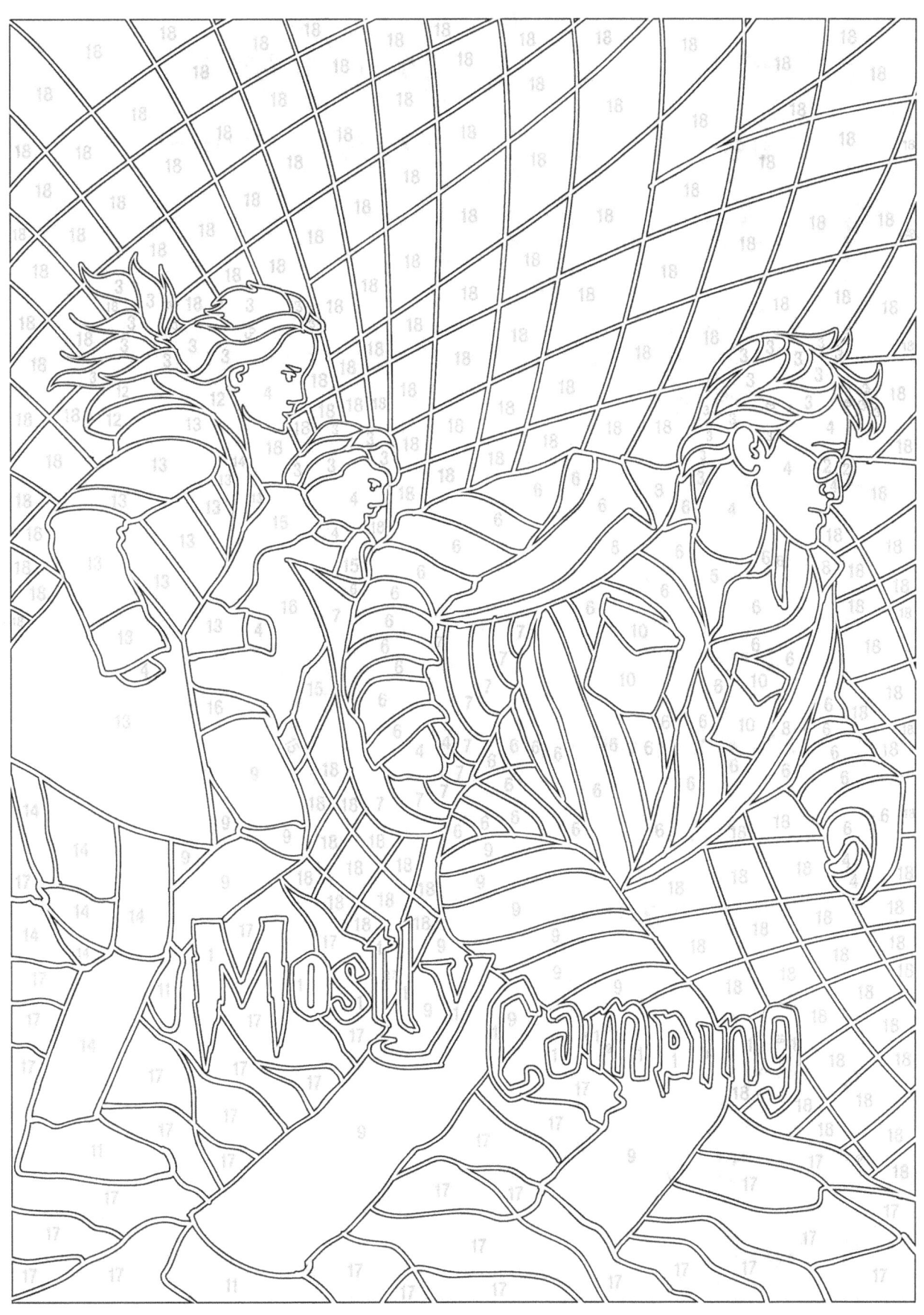

1. Red
2. Blue
3. Violet
4. Black
5. Orange
6. Gray
7. Dark Gray
8. White
9. Dark Brown
10. Brown
11. Dark Orange
12. Dark Red
13. Yellow
14. Light Pink
15. Blue
16. Light Blue
17. Baby Blue

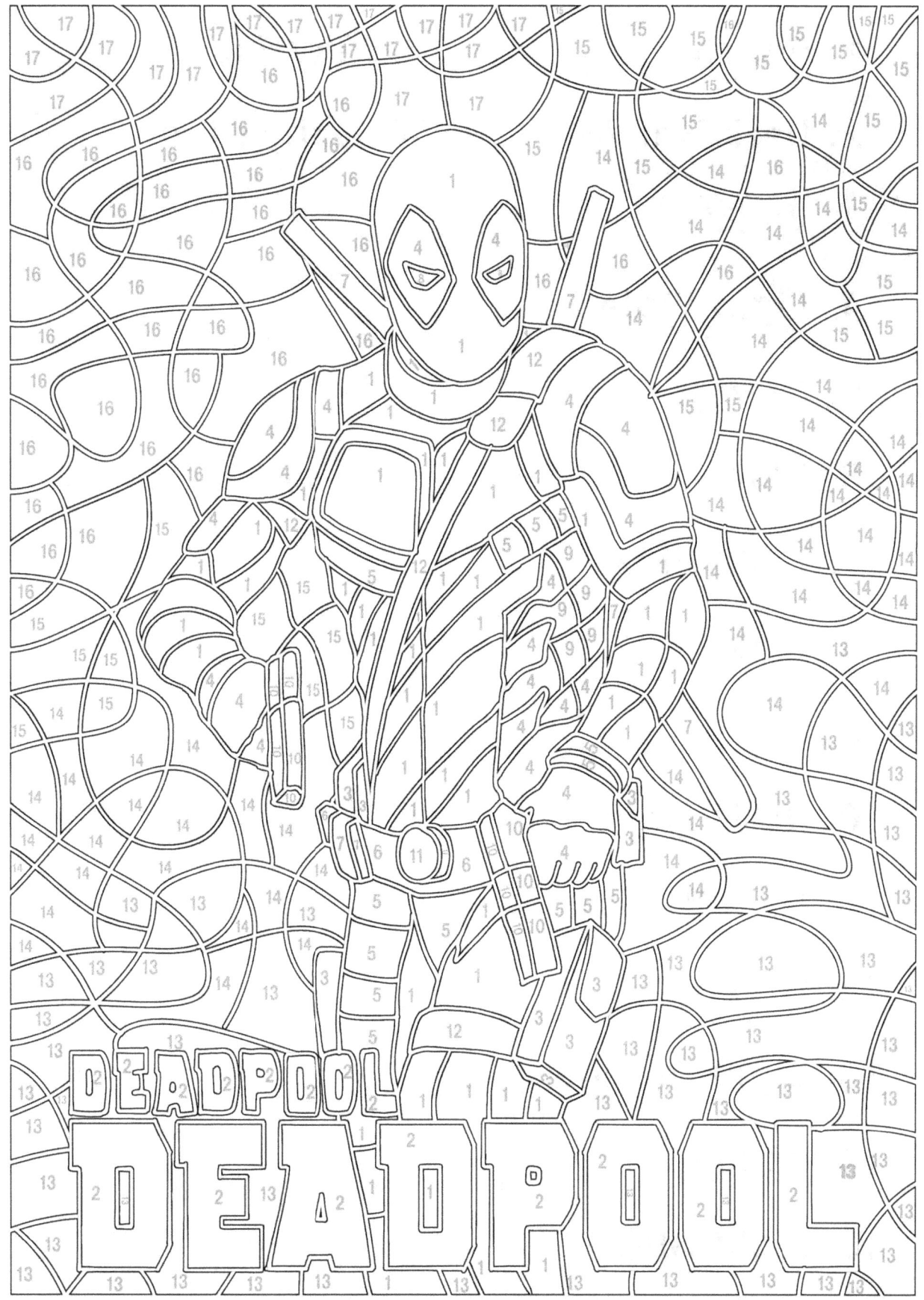

1. Peach
2. Dark Brown
3. Violet
4. Light Violet
5. Orange
6. Blue
7. Light Pink
8. Pink
9. Red
10. Dark Gray
11. Dark Blue
12. Green
13. Light Orange
14. Yellow
15. Light Blue
16. Sky Blue
17. Baby Blue

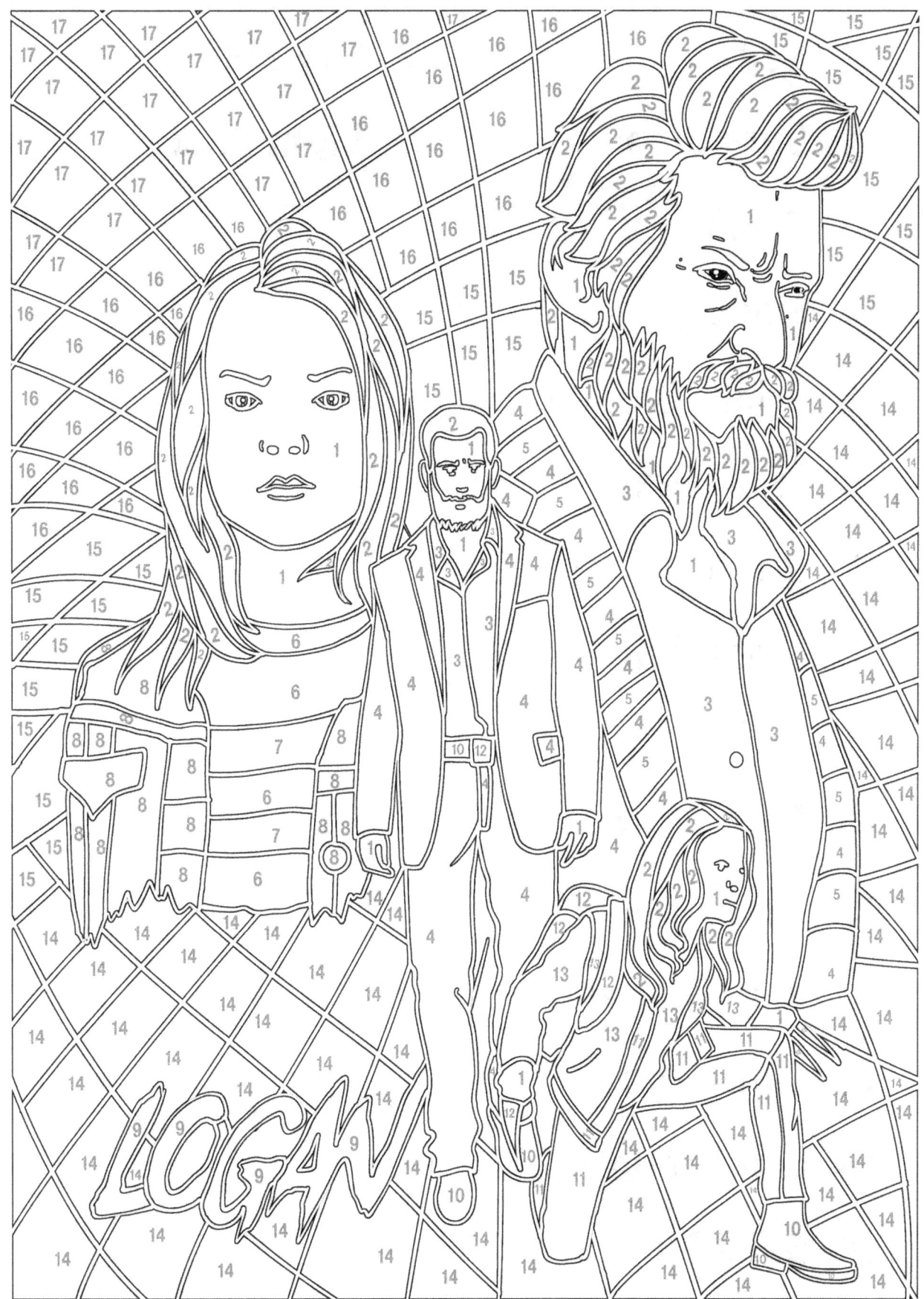

1. Red
2. Dark Blue
3. Black
4. White
5. Bright Orange
6. Light Gray
7. Medium Gray
8. Light Blue
9. Light Red
10. Dark Brown
11. Dark Gray
12. dark Orange
13. dark Yellow
14. Light Yellow
15. Baby Blue
16. Sky Blue
17. Light Pink

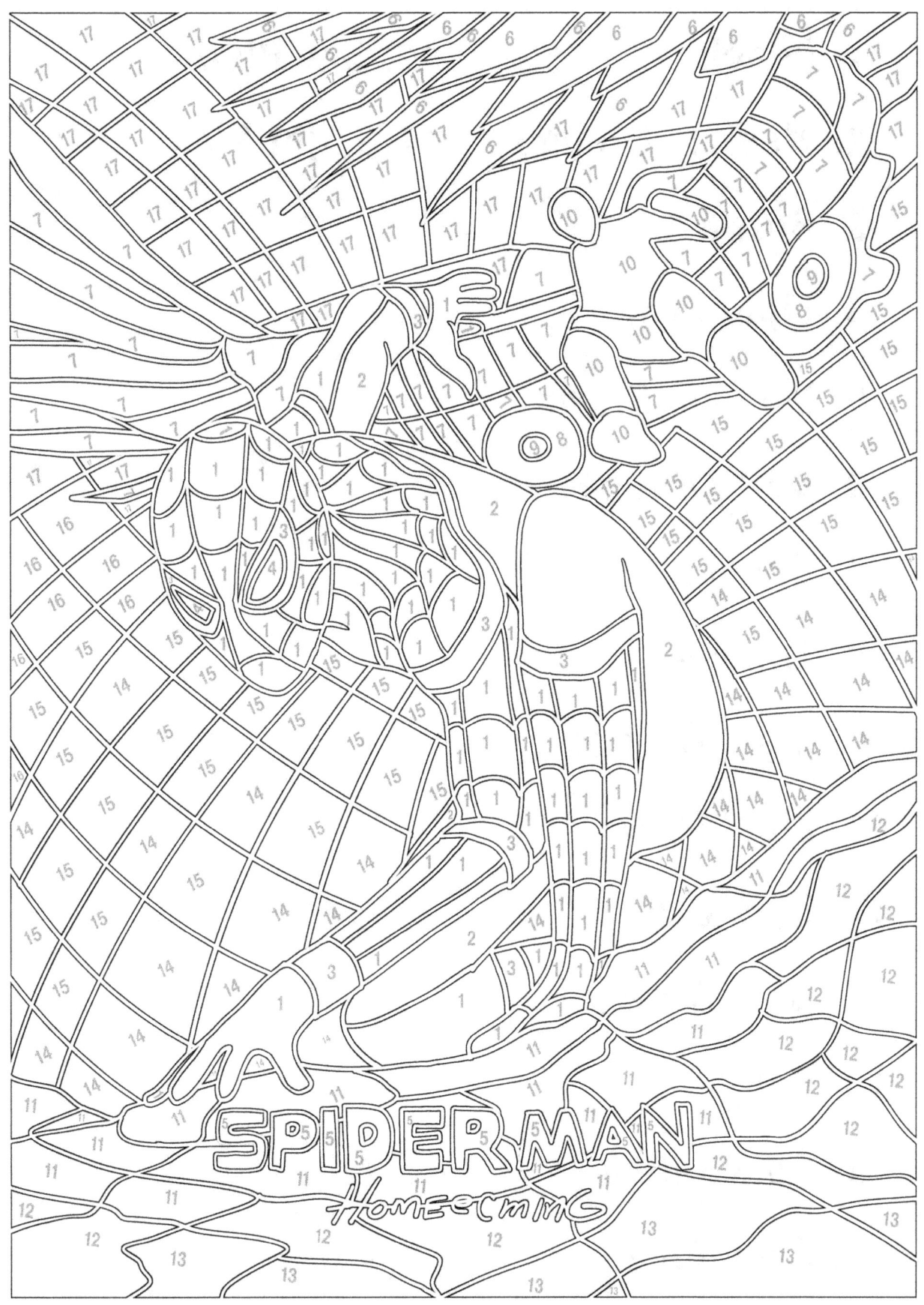

1. Peach
2. Medium Orange
3. Brown
4. Light Brown
5. Medium Brown
6. Dark Orange
7. Chocolate
8. Orange
9. Light Orange
10. Light Gray
11. Dark Gray
12. Dark Brown
13. Beige
14. Dark Yellow
15. Baby Blue
16. Sky Blue
17. Light Pink

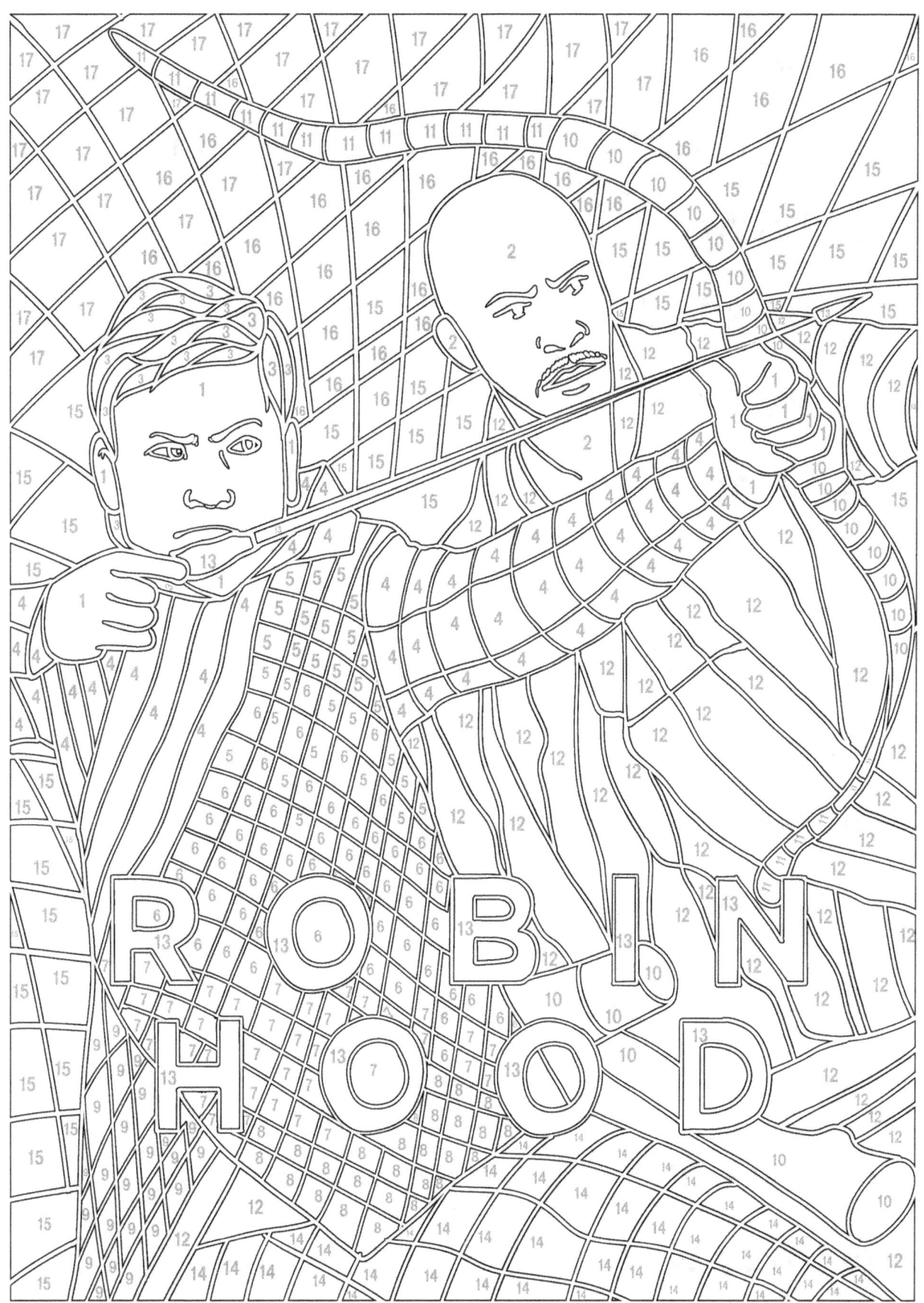

1. Red
2. Light Red
3. Yellow
4. Dark Red
5. Medium Red
6. Light Orange
7. Light Gray
8. Dark Gray
9. Brown
10. Medium Gray
11. Light Brown
12. Dark Orange
13. Beige
14. Dark Gray
15. Baby Blue
16. Sky Blue
17. Light Yellow

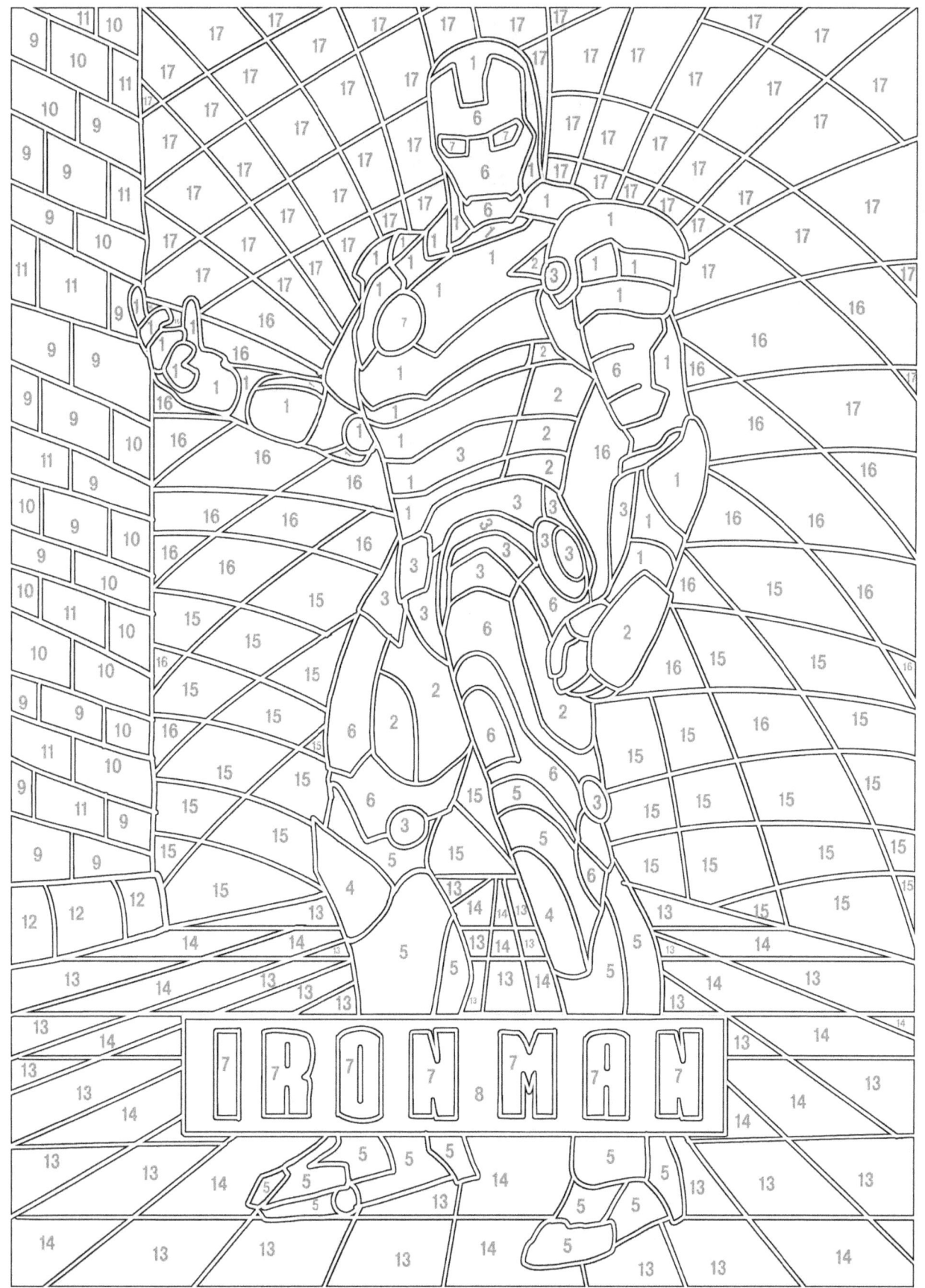

ENJOY BONUS IMAGES FROM SOME OF OUR OTHER FUN COLOR BY NUMBER BOOKS!

FIND ALL OF OUR BOOKS ON AMAZON

Dragon Fantasy
Mosaic Color By Number
Mythical Magic and Lore for Stress Relief

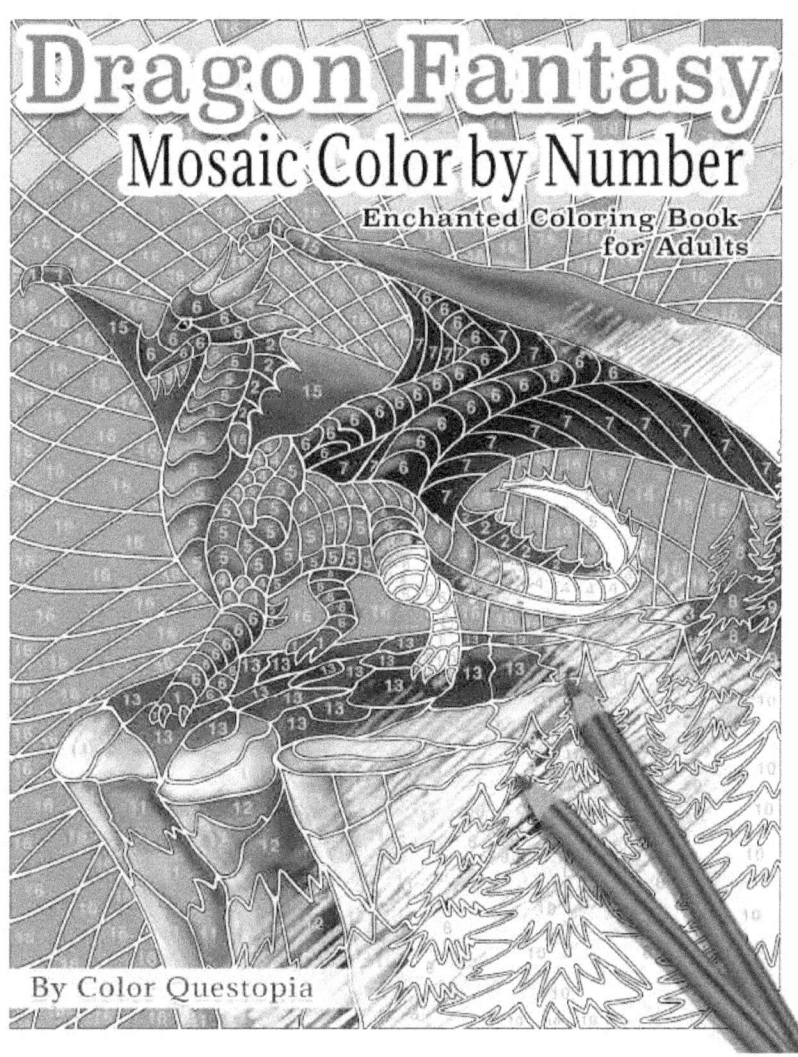

1. White
2. Dark Brown
3. Light Orange
4. Dark Yellow
5. Dark Red
6. Medium Orange
7. Army Green
8. Medium Brown
9. Red
10. Brown
11. Light Brown
12. Dark Gray
13. Medium Gray
14. Light Gray
15. Gray
16. Blue
17. Light Blue

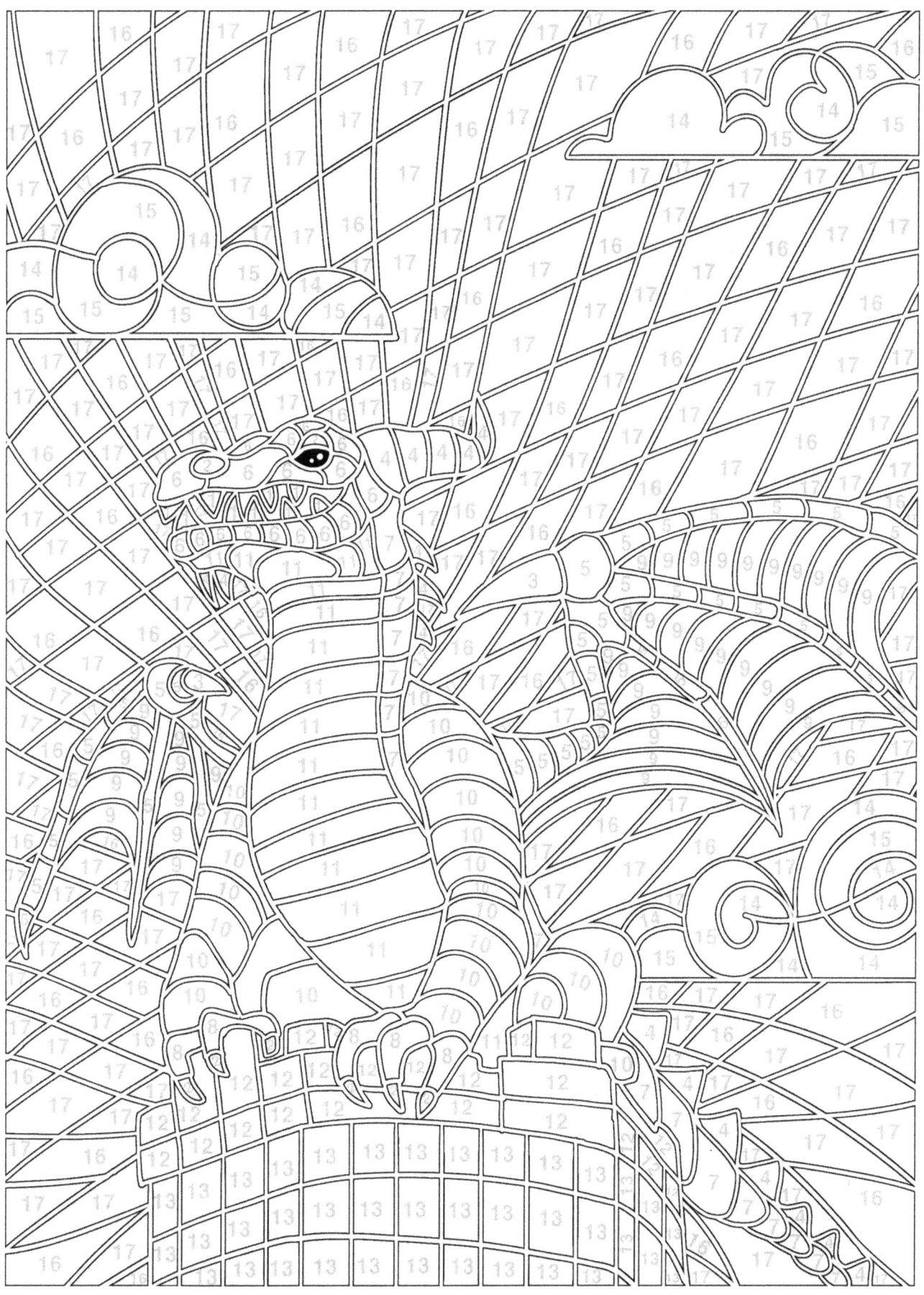

Color Quest Color By Number Animals
by Color Questopia

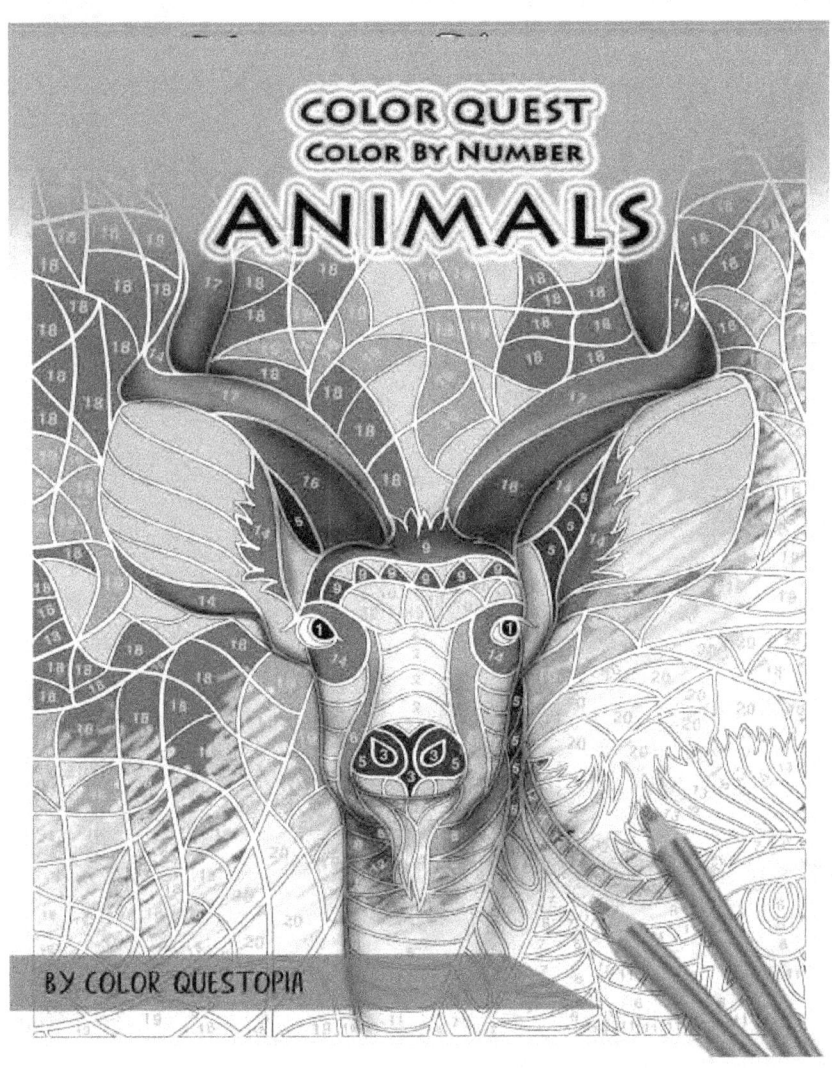

1. Black
2. Light Gray
3. Gray
4. Dark Brown
5. Light Violet
6. Orange
7. Light Yellow
8. Dark Orange
9. Brown
10. Dark Violet
11. Medium Purple
12. Green
13. Light Green
14. Neon Green
15. Yellow
16. Army Green
17. Violet
18. Dark Gray
19. Sky Blue
20. Light Pink

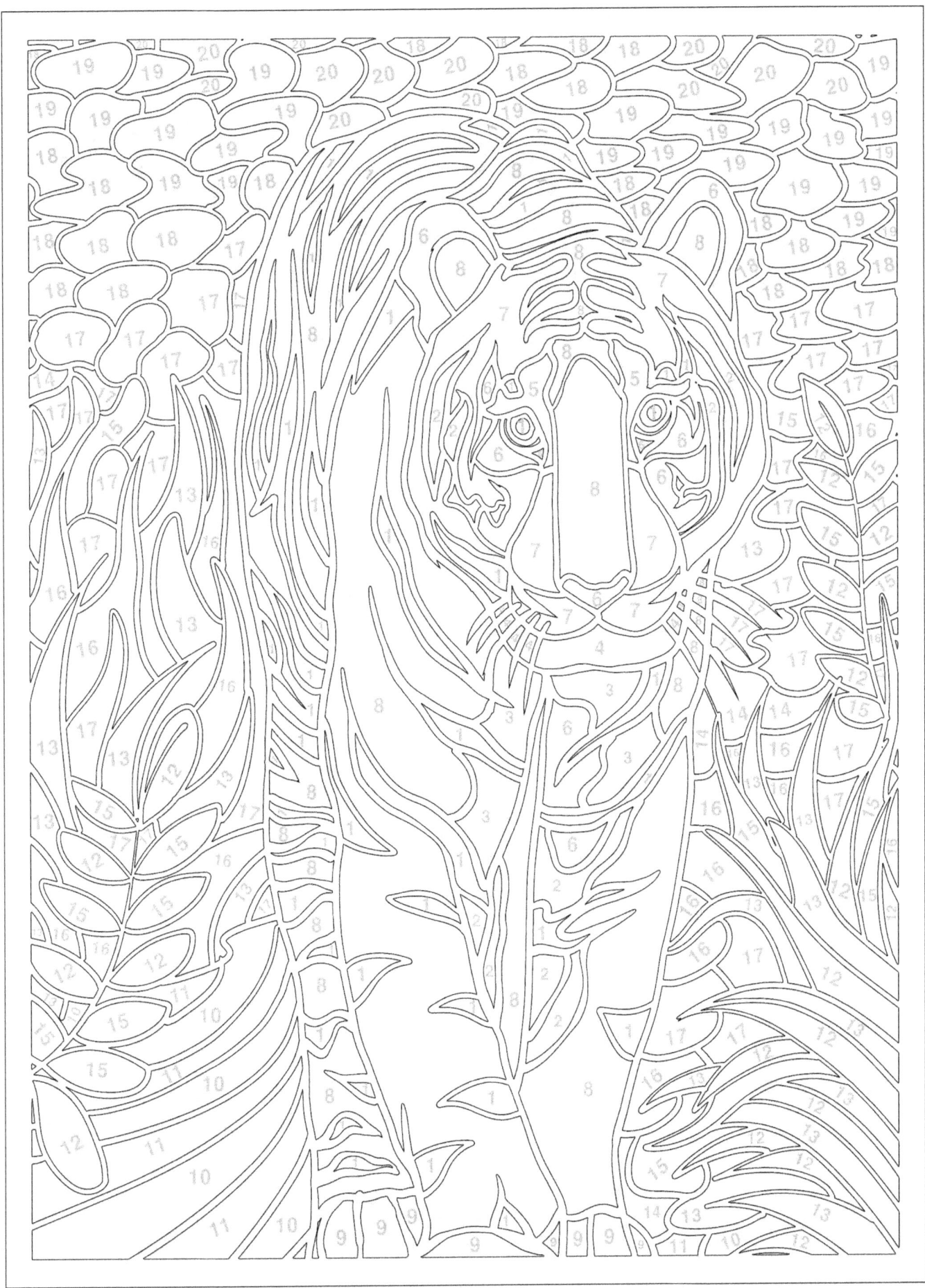

Fanciful Fox
Mosaic Adult Color by Number Book
Adult Coloring Book for Stress Relief
and Relaxation

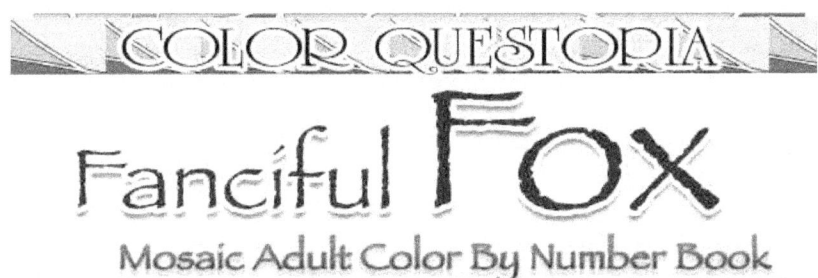

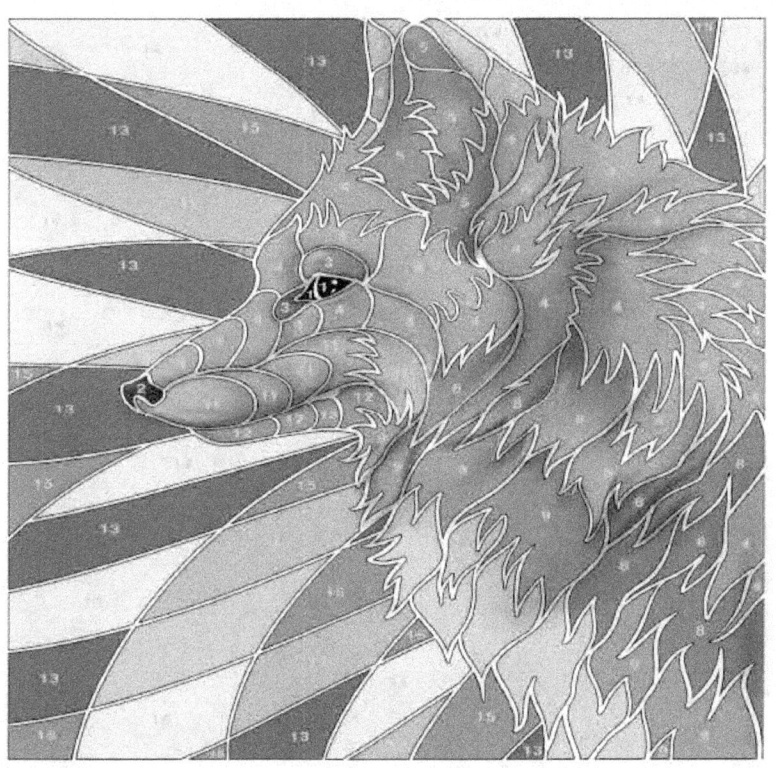

1. Black
2. Dark Brown
3. Light Orange
4. Light Yellow
5. Light Brown
6. Orange
7. Beige
8. Dark Yellow
9. Medium Brown
10. Brown
11. Gray
12. Dark Gray
13. Light Green
14. Green
15. Medium Gray
16. Light Gray
17. Sky Blue

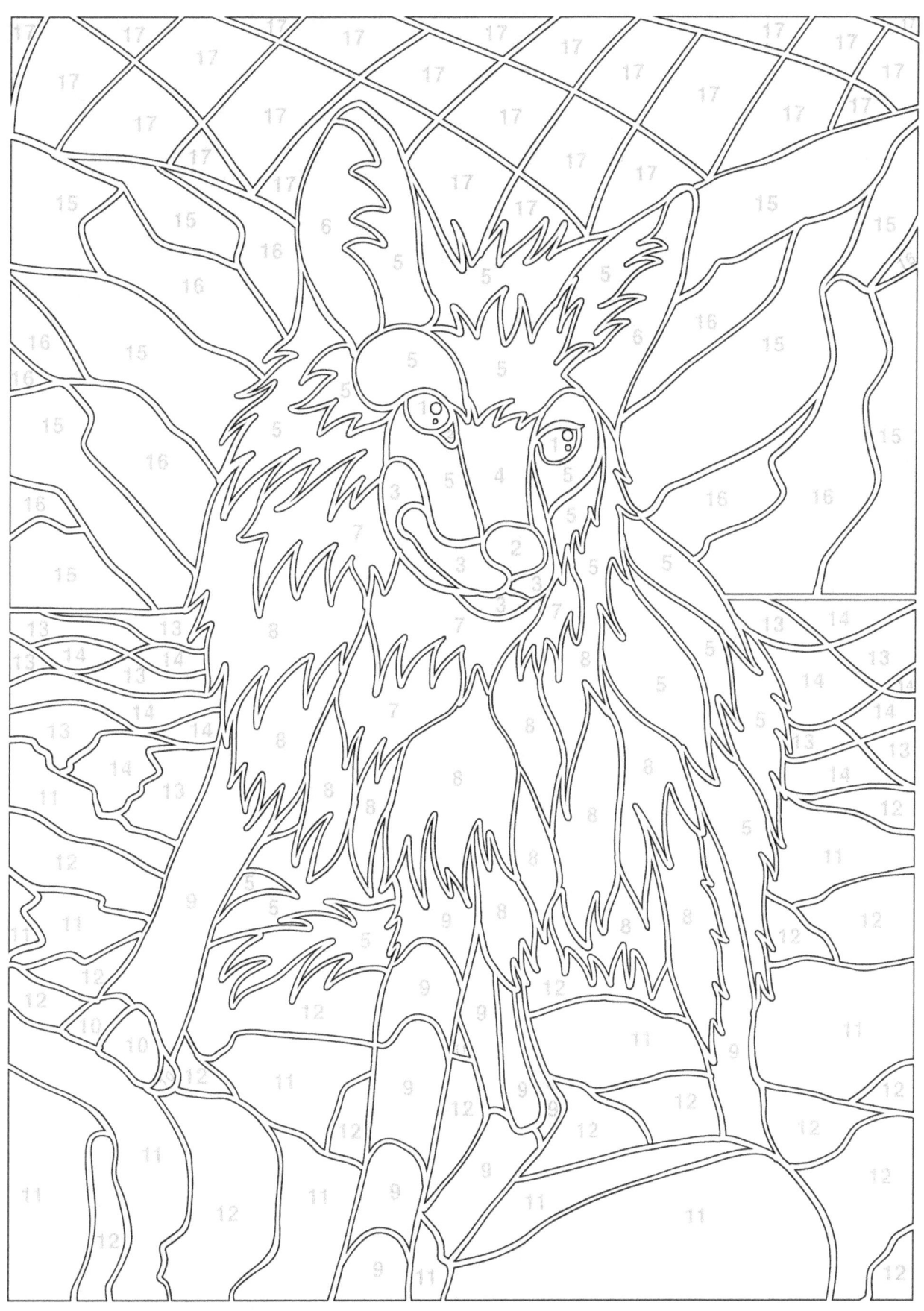

Beautiful Cities and Landmarks
Color by Number
Mosaic World Geography
Coloring Book For Adults

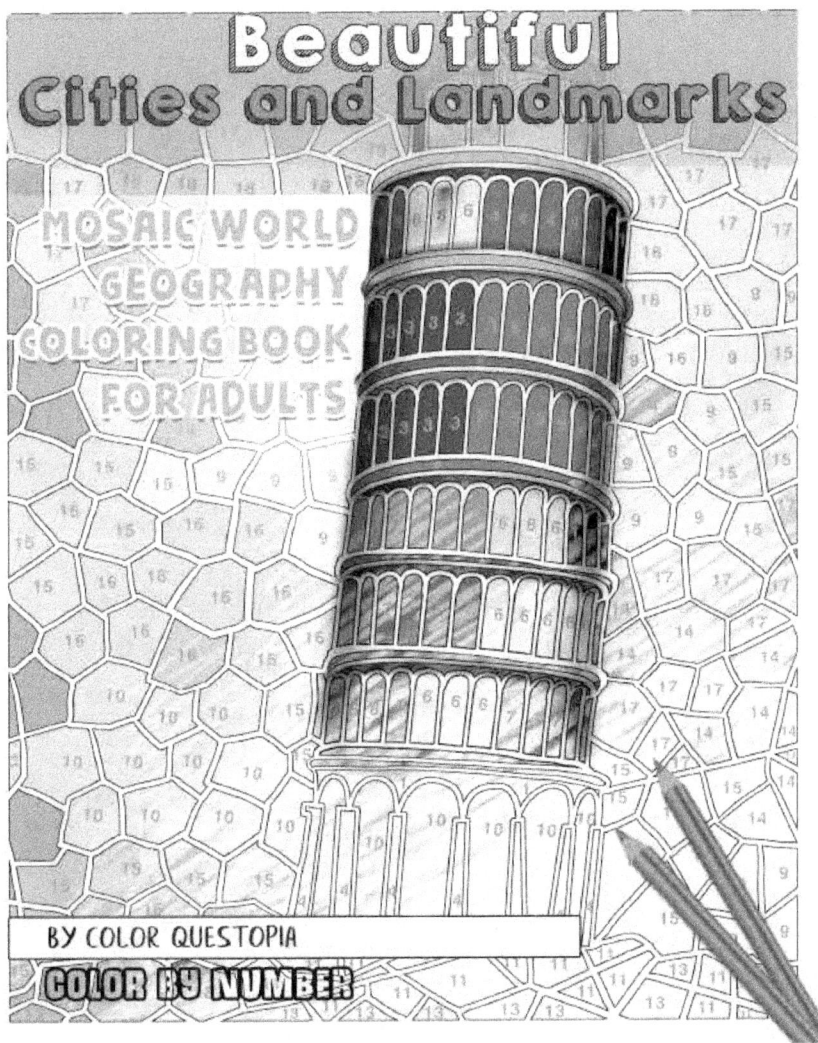

1. Light Green
2. Bright Orange
3. Orange
4. Dark Yellow
5. Dark Orange
6. Dark Red
7. Beige
8. Red
9. Deep Green
10. Navy Blue
11. Baby Blue
12. Light Pink
13. Hot Pink
14. Blue
15. Light Violet
16. Green
17. Yellow

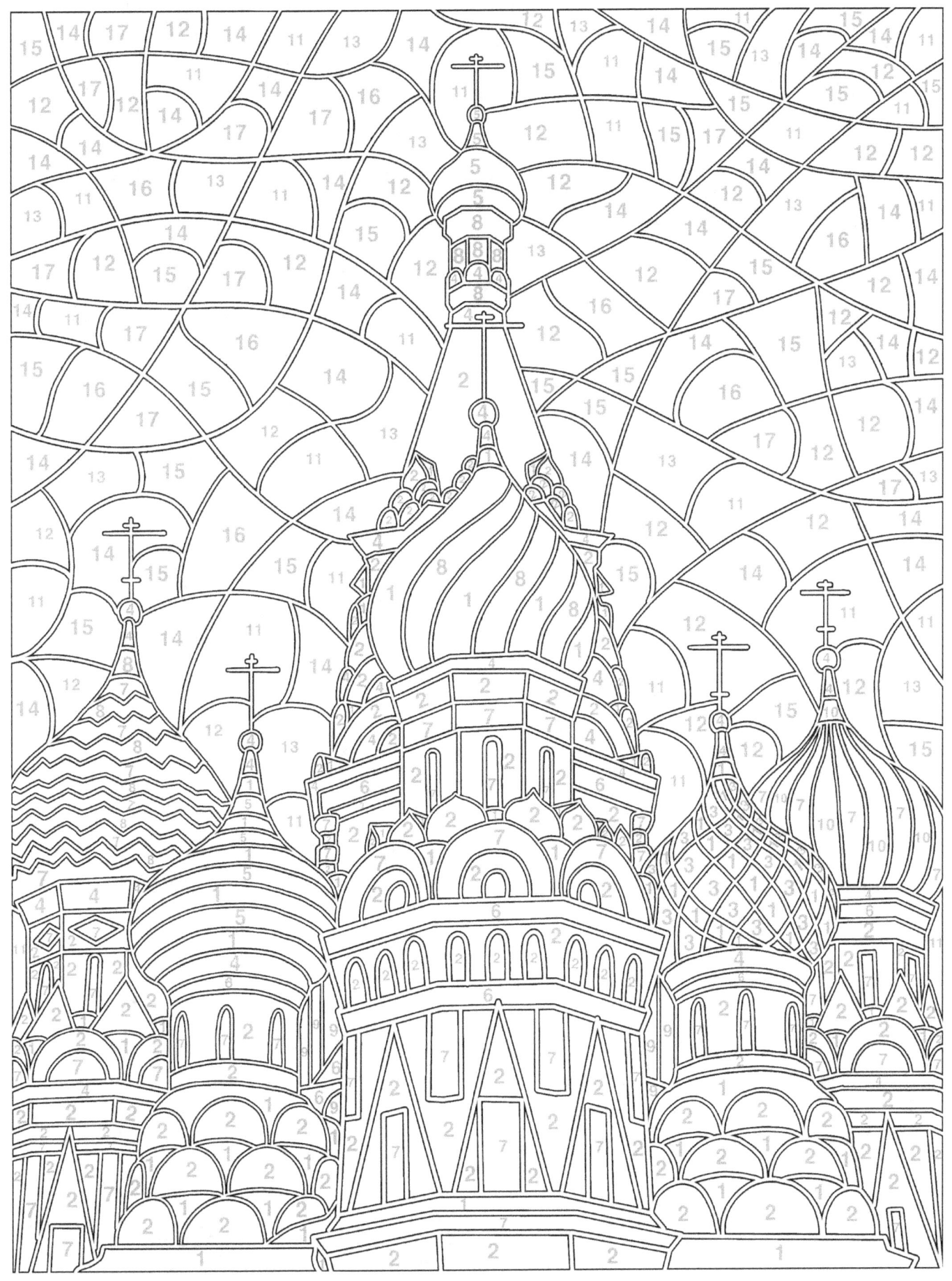

Horses Jumbo Adult Coloring Book
Horses and Ponies Grazing and Racing
Color by Number

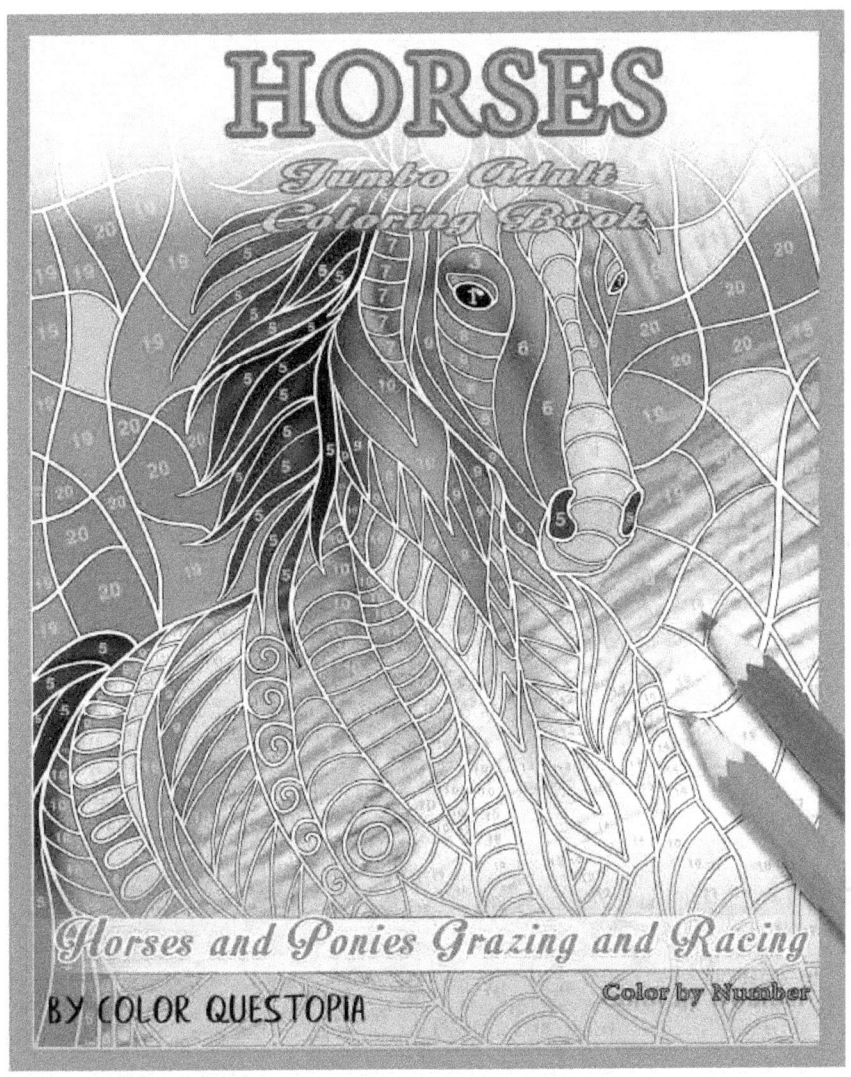

1. Black
2. Brown
3. Dark Brown
4. Light Brown
5. Red
6. Light Yellow
7. Dark Yellow
8. Dark Red
9. Gray
10. Light Gray
11. Medium Purple
12. Soft Violet
13. Dark Blue
14. Medium Green
15. Light Green
16. Deep Green
17. Dark Yellow
18. Yellow
19. Orange
20. Light Orange
21. Pink

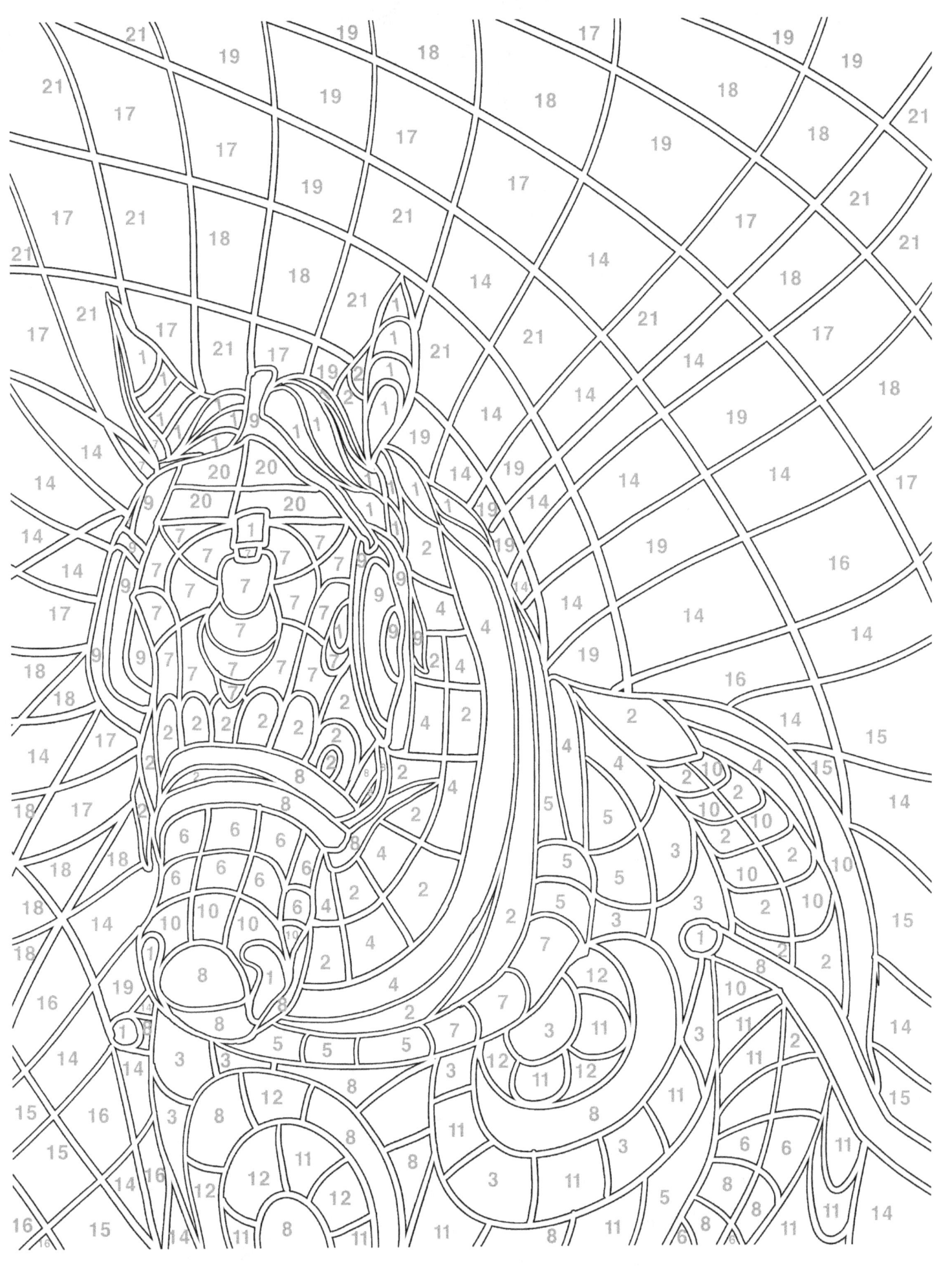

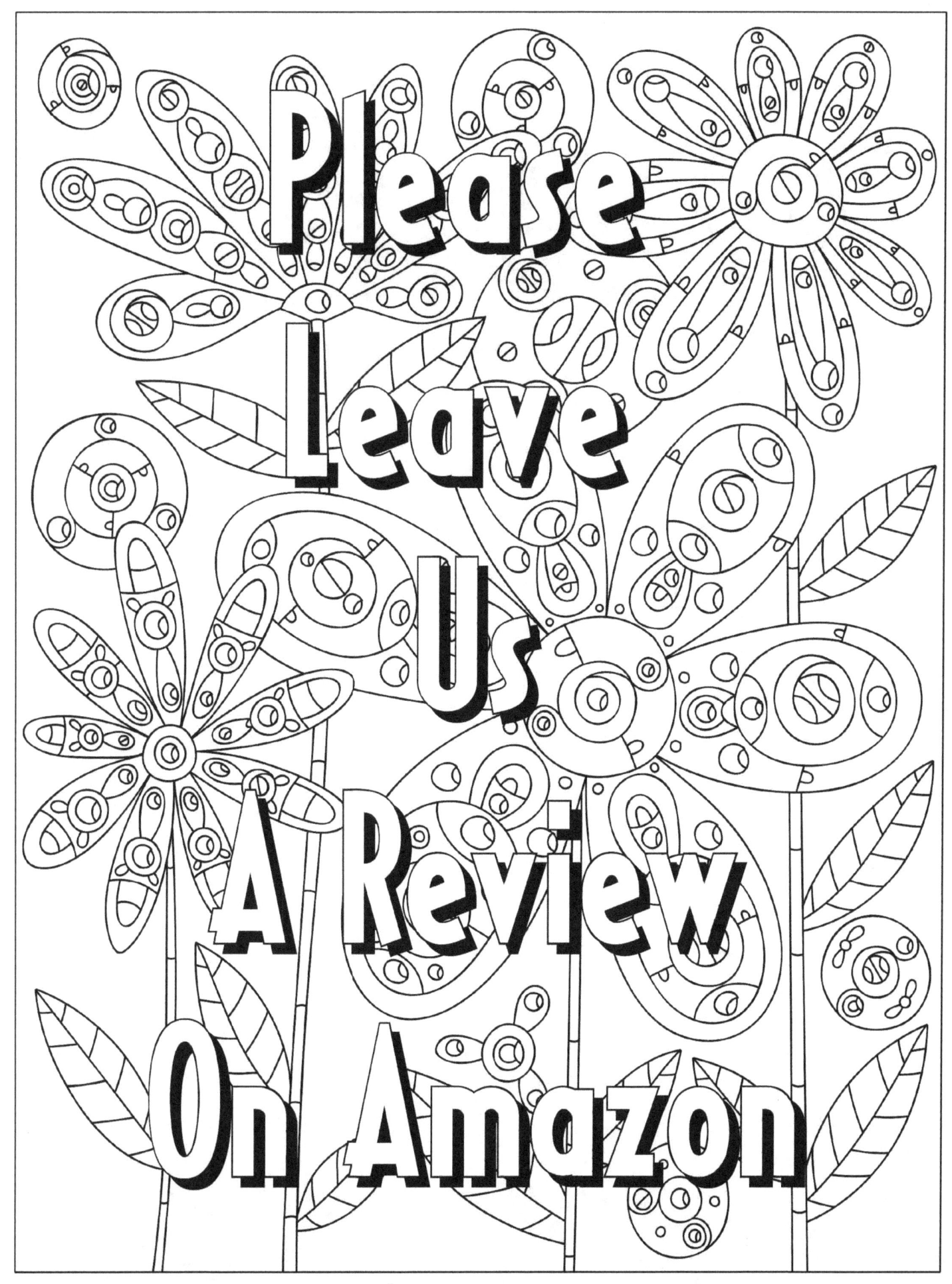

www.ingramcontent.com/pod-product-compliance
Lightning Source LLC
Chambersburg PA
CBHW080527220526
45465CB00006B/2623